– WILLIE'S STORY –

"Throughout our lives we program ourselves to react to our environment. Myself, well, I sort of overdid the anger bit. I had a very uneasy home life, and after several books and workbooks on anger, I was referred to Dr. Barris' anger-management group. He tells us he's writing a book: 'When Chicken Soup Isn't Enough,' and I think, 'Oh no, more gobbeldy-goop to mix me up again.' Then I think the group has been helpful, so I buy the book. It isn't complicated; in fact, it reads pretty well (for a psychology book, amazingly well). You see, I'm a maintenance engineer and this is not what I would usually read.

The book is sort of like an anger-management owners manual with homework. You learn to 'do-it-yourself.' After all, you're the one who angers yourself anyway. 'Turn your anger into irritation,' Dr. Barris says, and he shows you how. Look at all your options. Think before you react. There will be times when you get angry, but if you practice reasoning through the worksheets every day, you will become less and less angry.

I would recommend this book for all Employee Assistance Programs (EAPs), unions, Human Resource departments and managers. It's a good reference for couples before they marry. Youth leaders in schools and churches would benefit by sharing the contents of this book with our young people.

Anger is rampant. We are killing ourselves (blood pressure, nerves, etc.) and we are killing each other because we are losing control of our anger. This book is a fine tool to help you lessen your anger. Who knows, maybe then we can all learn to just get along with each other again."

Willie C.
Memphis, TN

When Chicken Soup Isn't Enough

Managing Your Anger in an Increasingly Angry World

Author's note: The ideas, suggestions, etc., presented in this book are not intended to be a substitute for consulting a professional therapist or counselor. All matters regarding your physical, psychological, or emotional health require professional supervision.

This book is dedicated to my beautiful wife
Valerie
whose encouragement of my efforts,
and acceptance of my many idiosyncrasies,
brings joy to my life.

TABLE OF CONTENTS

FOREWORD

Make no mistake about it, people who have difficulty managing their anger are in significant psychological pain and interpersonal despair. Though anger appears to help them get what they demand, they also understand that the costs of their anger far outweigh any imagined benefits. Angry people reading this book know that what I am saying is true because they live daily with the consequences of their anger. I understand how great the personal and interpersonal costs are because I, too, have experienced them.

When conducting seminars on managing anger I frequently begin by noting that "We often teach that which we need most to learn." If that statement is true, then working with people to help them overcome their anger problems is exactly what I need to be doing. It is important to me that you, the reader, appreciate that this book works on two levels. On one level I have tried basing my recommendations concerning the management of anger on the current "state of the art" research in this area. On a second, more deeply personal level, my hope is that you view the suggestions made in this book as an outgrowth of my work with hundreds of clients over the years, as well as my own daily struggles with anger—a struggle I anticipate continuing until my dying breath.

Though anger is an emotion we all experience, surprisingly little has been written about it. This is both a bane and a boon. It is a bane in that there are few established trails to follow in this area making the outcome of this entire enterprise riskier, more speculative and less sure. It is a boon for exactly the same reasons since the entire field of helping others manage their anger is open to exploration by those willing to undertake the journey. My most sincere hope is that this book provides a clear and precise map, devoid of unnecessary "psycho-babble," for helping you acquire the skills needed to better manage your anger.

We live in a world where bookstore shelves are crammed full of self-help titles promising all manner of benefit. Many shout about empowering the reader in some way (e.g., to overcome poor childhood experiences, to stop smoking or eating excessively). Though I am generally loathe to use that term, ultimately this book is about empowering yourself by helping you manage an emotion which, to this point, may have seemed beyond both your understanding and control. This book is about putting you in command of your emotional life by helping you *choose an emotion, other than anger, that allows you be more assertive, solve more of life's problems, as well as being a better friend, parent and partner.*

Once you develop a sense of mastery over your anger, your world will never be the same. I guarantee it!

ACKNOWLEDGEMENTS

Understanding the nature and treatment of anger has long been an interest of mine, so it is no surprise that this book has been kicking around in my head for many years. The wisdom I have developed to undertake such a project, such that it exists, is the end product of observations shared by countless group members and individual clients over many years. It is also the result of considerable self-reflection, coupled with superlative mentoring during my many years of clinical training.

To the extent that I possess the technical skills necessary to conduct both efficient and effective Rational Emotive Behavior Therapy (REBT) with my clients, I am deeply indebted to Ed Nottingham, Ph.D. His ability to utilize this mode of therapy, coupled with his ability to teach others how to use it, is unequalled in my experience.

To the extent that I have melded the techniques of REBT with the compassion of more constructivist, existential and humanistic approaches, I am deeply indebted to Robert Neimeyer, Ph.D. One of my dearest friends, he challenges me to always take into account the profoundly human dimensions of therapy.

I also need to acknowledge the contributions of my first mentor in this field, Joe Becker, Ph.D., who had the courage and compassion to make me aware of how anger was interfering with my journey through this world. He not only brought to my awareness how anger had become a pervasive and destructive part of my life, but he also stood beside me as I began to tackle this personal *bete noire*.

The contributions of Susan Mullikin, R.N., who has shared her warmth and wisdom with me over the years, have been legion. Despite our ups and downs, she remains a friend for all time.

My editor, Adam Anderson, kept me focused, especially throughout the final stages of this project. What a brilliant career as both a therapist and researcher lies ahead of him. Though I accept full responsibility for all errors remaining in this book, Adam's feedback was absolutely indispensable to the completion of this project.

Lastly, I need to acknowledge the contributions of my mother, Mercedes H. Barris. Her amazing common sense and wisdom are sprinkled liberally throughout these pages. She remains the most influential "disciple" in my life.

To each of these people I express my most heartfelt gratitude.

WHEN CHICKEN SOUP
ISN'T ENOUGH

CHAPTER ONE

WHY IS MANAGING ANGER SO DIFFICULT?

Life is difficult. This is a great truth, one of the greatest truths. It is a great truth because once we truly see this truth, we transcend it. Once we truly know that life is difficult--once we truly understand and accept it--then life is no longer difficult. Because once it is accepted, the fact that life is difficult no longer matters.

The Road Less Traveled, M. Scott Peck, M.D.

The same can be said of managing anger. As with life generally, managing anger is difficult. But, as I have learned over the years, once you accept that managing your anger will be a challenge, the fact that it is no longer matters.

Managing anger is difficult for many reasons. For some, anger appears to work. As they get angrier, and people give in to their demands, the angry person makes the mental connection that it was their anger that *made* others do what they demanded. Conveniently forgetting that others have freedom of choice, they convince themselves that anger helped them achieve their goals.

Managing anger is difficult because anger is "overlearned." If I asked you to tie your shoelace for me, and then asked whether or not you had thought about tying your shoelace, chances are you would say "no." Upon reflection, however, it wouldn't be possible to execute the series of hand, leg and foot maneuvers required to tie a shoelace unless there were instructions going from your brain to various parts of your body. The reason you would answer "no" is because the sequences of thoughts associated with tying your shoelace are overlearned, or automatic. You will soon learn that your thoughts associated with getting angry are also quite automatic.

Managing anger is difficult because, for some, anger helps them hold on to the past, even an unpleasant past. Not unlike other negative emotions such as clinical depression or high levels of anxiety, anger can keep us connected to people no longer in our lives.

My grandmother divorced her husband during the early 1920's--something unheard of at that time. Until her death in 1995, "That bastard Charlie..." preceded every negative comment she made. For over sixty years she held on to her anger and, in so doing, kept alive the memory of their relationship. Though he died years before her, my grandmother's anger toward "That bastard Charlie..." burned in her heart until the day she died.

Managing anger can be difficult because some people view anger as a more acceptable emotional response than feelings of hurt, sadness, guilt or shame. When was the last time you heard a husband acknowledge to his male companions feeling hurt or sad over his wife leaving him for another man? How many people do you know who, having been caught doing something they know they shouldn't, convert their shame and guilt into anger and then blame others for discovering them? Other emotions can be easily converted into anger when it serves an individual's purposes.

Managing anger is challenging because anger appears to be a universal emotional experience. No matter where on earth you go, anger is one of a limited number of basic human emotions. Albert Ellis, the architect of Rational Emotive Behavior Therapy (REBT), suggests that humans are genetically predisposed to think in ways that produce negative emotions, of which anger is but one. Whether anger is a genetic problem, or a problem associated with one's upbringing, is ultimately not important. What is important, however, is accepting the reality that we all experience anger at some point in our lives.

> *During my anger management seminars I often ask if there is any one in the audience who doesn't get angry. Invariably someone will raise his or her hand. At which point I respond, "Well, that's very interesting because if you look in the Bible even Jesus got angry on various occasions. If you are doing better than Jesus did, perhaps you and I can get together after the seminar to talk some more!"*

Traditionally, researchers have studied seven basic human emotions: shame, guilt, disgust, joy, sadness, fear and anger. Recent work by Dr. Ray DiGiuseppe and his colleagues, summarizing cross-cultural studies on anger, has identified those characteristics that make anger so difficult to tame.

> -Anger is experienced *more frequently* than other emotions. During the course of the day, which emotion do you experience more often, shame, guilt, disgust, joy, sadness, fear or anger? For many, anger is the emotion chosen most frequently.

> -Anger is as *intense as fear* and includes *high sympathetic nervous system arousal*. With the activation of the sympathetic nervous system comes the release of adrenaline leading some people to report that they get "high" on their anger. This is how anger can become "addictive" for certain people.

> -Anger *lasts longer* than other emotional states. How long does it take you to cool down after getting angry? Once you get angry you will tend to stay that way for an extended period of time. This is a consequence of both your faulty thinking, as well as how your body deals with anger.

-Anger produces a *strong tendency to approach, rather than avoid, the person or situation your anger is directed toward.* When you get angry with someone, do you avoid him or her or do you "get up in his or her face?" While some people get angry and retreat, most tend to move toward the person with whom they are angry. This may have something to do with the next characteristic of anger.

-Anger includes an *experience of greater power or potency* than do the other emotions. The last time you were angry with your someone, didn't you feel powerful relative to him or her? Since we perceive of ourselves as powerful when we're angry, it makes sense that we would want to confront the person our anger is directed towards.

-*Joy is the only emotion people are less likely to want to change than anger.* Were it not for problems at home, at work or with the legal system, would you really want to control your anger? Most likely not.

What does all this mean? It means that trying to control your anger involves asking yourself to give up what is likely your most frequent, intense and long lasting emotional experience. It's suggesting that you abandon an emotion that gives you a feeling of power and potency. It means giving up on the almost addictive quality of anger which, like other addictions, feels--at least for the moment--so good!

> *Willie, an anger management group member, observed, "You know, I've been addicted to everything. Alcohol, cocaine, you name it. I never realized that what I was really addicted to is my anger. When I get angry I feel good and, the thing is, I don't have to pay anything for it. It's free! And I can give myself a fix whenever I want it. The only problem is that I'm 47 years-old now, have three kids, and I'm sick and tired of feeling that way any more."*

And yet many people just like you *do* change by challenging what seems natural, and even pleasurable, to become less angry. Why? Because, despite all the seeming advantages and pleasures anger brings, there are also some painful costs. Some of those costs are captured in the following hard truths about anger.

UNDERSTANDING ANGER: THE HARD TRUTHS

Anger can kill you. Research clearly demonstrates that persons unable to manage their anger are at greater risk for heart disease, high blood pressure, headaches, strokes and stomach-related problems. A recent study suggests that persons reporting higher levels of anger at age twenty-five are four to seven times more likely to be dead by age fifty than those persons reporting lower levels of anger!

These physical problems set the stage for a type of drawn out, slow motion "dance of death" whereby anger, over time, robs you of health and, ultimately, your life.

In addition to the physical toll chronic anger takes on your body, there is the toll it takes on people or things around you. Angry people often behave aggressively towards others, e.g., yelling, hitting things, hitting other people, etc. All you need do is read the morning paper, or watch the evening news, to know that aggression begets aggression. In a world where people frequently carry weapons, aggressive behavior can cost you your life in the blink of an eye.

> *In high school I was notorious for my aggressive driving. One of my favorite tactics involved allowing the car behind me, with its high beams on, to pass. I would then "open up" on the driver (as if I was shooting him or her!) with a specially installed bank of driving lights that could illuminate a city block. When I told my mother about this brilliant behavior she responded, "You know Brad, one of these days you're going to do that to someone and they're going to pull up next to you and put a bullet in your head. I know you think you're invincible, but you're not!"*

Anger destroys your most important relationships. No one enjoys being around an angry person. Just ask your ex-wife or husband, or that ex-employer. Just ask your son or daughter as they nervously avoid your touch and politely decline your invitation to join in opening Christmas presents. Like no other emotion, anger pushes others away, isolating you from them and from the world.

Society punishes angry people who behave aggressively. In his commentary on the poem "There Was A Little Girl" from *The Book of Virtues*, William J. Bennett makes the following observation:

> *[In the poem] we meet the child who, like most, is sometimes well behaved and sometimes not. And we face a hard, unavoidable fact of life: if we cannot control our own behavior, eventually someone will come and control it for us in a way we probably will not like.*

If you are unable to manage your anger, and the aggressive behaviors growing out of that anger society, through its legal mechanisms, will attempt to control your anger for you--most likely in ways you will not like. The batterer intervention groups I conduct are a perfect example of persons who are being punished by society for their anger and resulting aggressive behaviors. No matter how self-righteous or justified you might believe your anger to be, society will punish you, especially if your anger turns into aggression.

Life will find ways to punish you for being angry. This is a somewhat philosophical observation but one that angry people understand almost immediately.

Opportunities that may have materialized, had you been less angry, pass you by. Doors that may have opened, because of your skills or knowledge, remain closed because others fear being exposed to your excessive anger. Mysteriously or not, life has a way of evening the score because angry people give life the means by which they are ultimately humbled.

> *Tony buys used cars for auto dealers. He announced to the group that he had gone to an auction over the weekend and had "told off" the auctioneer who, apparently, had passed him over during the bidding on a particularly desirable car. "God, I was so mad! And it felt so good to tell the SOB off! The problem is he won't let me back in to the auction and, if I can't buy cars there, I'm out of a job."*

THE LIES WE TELL OURSELVES TO JUSTIFY OUR ANGER

People are masters at lying to themselves in order to justify, or validate, their anger. They lie to themselves because they understand, almost unconsciously, that their anger is an outgrowth of faulty thinking that not only harms them, but also everyone and everything they hold dear. What follows is only a partial listing of the lies people tell themselves in order to justify their anger.

LIE #1: *"If I don't get angry, and behave aggressively, people will think I'm a wimp and walk all over me."*

In our culture, few interpersonal styles are viewed as negatively as being labeled passive or a "wimp." Many people rely on getting angry, and then behaving aggressively, as a way of countering the perceptions of others that they are weak. The problem with this approach is that, if someone is determined to view you as weak, all the anger and aggression you can generate will not necessarily change his or her view of you. As a matter of fact, others will actually point to your anger as proof that you are weak and out of control! As you will learn, being able to choose your emotional responses, including ones other than anger, are signs of strength, not weakness.

LIE #2: *"I just get angry. Emotions are things over which I have no control."*

The notion of being able to *choose* your emotional response in a particular situation at first sounds strange. Throughout our lives we have been taught that emotions are things that *happen to us* and, as such, are beyond our control. Nothing, however, could be further from the truth. Emotions, as you will learn, are products of how you think in specific situations. To the extent that you control your thinking so, too, can you exercise control over your emotions. By using the techniques you will learn in this book, you will no longer be a prisoner of unhelpful emotions like anger.

LIE #3: *"Only by expressing my anger am I going to feel better. I should never keep my anger bottled up!"*

Growing up during the 1960's and 70's, I heard popular psychologists and others in the media warn that the worst thing you could do was keep your anger "in." Unfortunately, an entire generation seems to have concluded that if keeping anger in is "bad," then letting it out must surely be "good." If you are unhappy about the world we currently live in understand that it is, in large part, a product of persons following the advice to always let their anger out.

I have a mental image of the dangers associated with keeping my anger bottled up. Like steam in a covered pot, the pressure would build until my skull started to expand. Once the natural limits of that expansion had been reached, my head would begin slowly turning, eventually gaining speed until it finally separated from my shoulders and launched into space--all because I had kept my anger in! What utter nonsense! While we have agreed that chronically angry people are more likely to experience certain physical problems than their non-chronically angry counterparts, that does not mean that the solution to your anger problem involves spewing anger out every time you experience it. The reality is that there are countless examples of persons you are better *not* expressing anger towards, including spouses, children, police officers, employers, judges and drunks brandishing guns!

Rather than struggling to keep anger "in," or surrendering to it by letting it "out," you need to learn to *manage* your anger so as to avoid both the physical problems associated with its repression, as well as the personal and interpersonal problems associated with its expression.

LIE #4: *"There is such a thing as healthy anger."*

I hear this often, even from colleagues who, because they were human beings long before they became therapists, are almost as reluctant as their clients to abandon a belief in the helpfulness of anger. As with other negative emotional experiences (i.e., clinical depression, elevated levels of anxiety), anger can be viewed as conveying information concerning the current state of one's psychological world. Anger can alert you to problems in your world that need to be solved. Used in this way, anger *can* be helpful and, in that respect, healthy.

Unfortunately, precious few people use their anger this way. The vast majority experience anger as I did in the following vignette. Since this is the way most people experience anger, I must respectfully disagree with my colleagues who believe in the notion of healthy anger. Instead, I believe there is such a thing as *healthy irritation* that helps you overcome life's problems, while intense feelings of anger will always cause you more problems.

6

I conducted a workshop for 200 professionals at a university based medical school. In order to illustrate my contention that there is no such thing as healthy anger, I recounted the story of how I infuriated myself while writing this book. Working under a deadline, I realized that all of the changes I had made to the manuscript went unsaved by my computer. I described calling my wife, yelling at her about the situation, and experiencing the most intense desire to throw the phone through the computer monitor. After twenty minutes of ranting and raving, I recomposed myself and began addressing the problem of recovering my lost work. Where is the "healthy anger" in this situation? As in all cases of anger, it is nowhere to be found.

LIE #5: *"Hitting something, like a pillow, will help me deal better with my anger."*

This is the "catharsis theory" of dealing with anger. It emphasizes "letting off steam" as the best way to deal with anger. Regretfully, there is no evidence to support the value of this approach. As a matter of fact, all the evidence supports that this is exactly the wrong way to learn anger control. In the case of hitting a pillow, you *will* feel better *immediately* after discharging your anger. This is the same sense of relief client's report after putting their fist through a wall or slamming a door. Unfortunately, rather than dealing with their anger in constructive ways, they are simply rehearsing future aggressive behaviors. In cases like this, the person recalls the momentary relief they experience after behaving aggressively. That split-second of relief reinforces their aggressive behavior and, as a consequence, they tend to behave this way in the future. This sense of immediate relief is also easily transferable from hitting inanimate objects to hitting people. You can see how this approach to dealing with anger may lead to significant new problems!

LIE #6: *"I can't help it if other people, or situations, make me angry!"*

This is the greatest lie of all, and the one that is the source of more personal and interpersonal suffering than any other. It is the lie that everyone reading this book believes, as surely as they know that the sun rises in the East and sets in the West. Everyone reading this book believes this lie because it's what he or she has always been taught. It's what we believe because we live in a world where, if we experience something unpleasant, like anger, then some one or some thing else must be the cause of, or to blame for, our discomfort.

How many times have you said to yourself, *"(Fill in the blank) makes me so angry!"* or *"I wouldn't have gotten angry if (fill in the blank) had done what he said he would do!"* Do you see any problems with believing that other people make you angry? As long as you believe that other people make you angry, *they are in control of your emotions!* As long as you believe that other people make you angry, *you are powerless over your anger!* To be in control of your emotional life, to regain your personal power, it is essential that you abandon the notion that others make you angry and replace it, instead, with the Rational Emotive Behavior Therapy (REBT) proposition that only *you* are powerful enough to create your own anger!

> *An image client's report to be helpful, as they struggle to free themselves from the belief that other people make them angry, involves that of a puppet-master and a puppet. As you know, the puppet-master manipulates and controls the puppet via a series of strings running from a cross-like device to the various parts of the puppet. As long as you believe that others make you angry, which are you, the puppet-master or the puppet? Obviously, you are the puppet. Getting out a pair of "psychological scissors" and cutting those strings so you can stand on your own, and accept responsibility for the creation of your anger, is what this book is all about.*

DEFINING TERMS: ANGER vs. IRRITATION

While anger is clearly an individual experience, its treatment requires that we agree upon a definition of this emotion that takes into account features common to all human beings. For the purposes of this book, *anger is defined as:*

> -the emotion humans experience when they do not get what they *think* they *should* or *must* get, or when they are denied what they believe they are *entitled* to.

> -the emotion humans experience when they are starkly confronted by the realization that they *cannot control others.*

> -the emotion that *activates the sympathetic nervous system* (e.g., increasing heart rate, increasing muscle tension, etc.) results in a significantly *increased likelihood of aggressive behavior* (either verbal or physical), and results in *seriously diminished problem solving, parenting skills* and *interpersonal relationships.*

Based on this definition, it's easy to understand why I disagree with colleagues and clients who argue that anger can be "healthy," or a positive emotional experience. From my perspective **anger is almost always bad for you!** If I am labeling anger as bad, and then asking you to abandon feeling angry to the greatest extent possible, it would be unfair of me to do so without proposing another emotion to take its place. The emotion I am proposing you replace anger with is *irritation*.

For the purposes of this book, *irritation is defined as:*

> -the emotion humans experience when they do not get what they *prefer, desire, hope, want,* or *wish* for.

8

-the emotion humans experience when they *accept that they cannot control others.*

-the emotion that results in little, if any, sympathetic nervous system arousal, leads to an *increased likelihood of assertive behavior,* as well as *improved problem solving, parenting skills* and *interpersonal relationships.*

Based on these definitions, your task in managing anger is to learn how to move from anger to irritation. The reasons why it is important to make that shift, and how to accomplish it, are discussed in the next chapter.

SUGGESTED HOMEWORK:

A.)   Describe two of the lies people tell themselves in order to justify their anger.

　　　1.)_____
　　　2.)_____

B.)   List two reasons why managing anger is difficult.

　　　1.)_____
　　　2.)_____

C.)   What are two of the "hard truths" associated with getting angry?

　　　1.)_____
　　　2.)_____

D.)   Contrary to popular belief, there is no such thing as _____ anger.

E.)   As long as you believe that _____you angry, you will always be the _____, and they will be the _____ _____.

F.)   The goal of anger management is to change_____into _____.

CHAPTER TWO

MANAGING ANGER: THE BASICS

God grant me the serenity
to accept the things I cannot change,
courage to change the things I can,
and the wisdom to know the difference.

Reinhold Niebuhr

Ours is a culture where people seek easy solutions to life's problems. Who amongst us wouldn't prefer taking a miracle pill in order to lose weight, rather than denying ourselves favorite foods and spending countless hours on health club treadmills? So, too, when it comes to managing anger, people look for the magic, effortless solution to their distress. Unfortunately, there is no miracle pill, or magic, effortless solution to the problem of your excessive anger. Those hoping that this book would offer such a simplistic solution need read no further.

While there are various ways to manage anger, the overwhelming first choice of most people is to *avoid the people who make them mad*. The problem with that strategy should be clear almost instantly. In the real world it is not always possible to avoid the people who make you mad. You will get angry with bosses, spouses, children, in-laws, co-workers, etc. It is unrealistic to expect that you would give up a high paying job, a long-standing marriage and contact with your children simply because you cannot control our anger towards them. Rather than avoiding these people, you need to change your angry responding to them.

Other ways of managing anger focus on addressing the physical dimensions of the problem. Books and programs emphasize various relaxation techniques and controlled breathing exercises as ways to reduce anger. While these approaches can be helpful, and will be covered in detail later in this book, they do not answer the basic question every angry person struggles with which is: "But why do I get so angry in the first place?"

This book answers that question in a way that makes sense to the vast majority of readers. The answer does not require that you look into the murky recesses of a past you cannot change, nor towards others in the present over whom you have no control. Rather, the question is answered by the following straightforward proposition:

It is not life's circumstances that make you angry. Rather, it is how you <u>choose</u> to think about those circumstances that causes your anger.

While the proposition itself is simple, understanding and applying it to your life is anything but!

WHERE ANGER COMES FROM: "SHOULDING-ON" OTHERS

Albert Ellis, through the principles of REBT, teaches that anger is not caused by the things that happen to us, or don't happen to us, but is the result of the universal, very human habit of elevating, in our minds,

the things we would *like* to have, *wish* to have, *hope* to have and *prefer* having

into

things we *believe* we MUST have, SHOULD have, OUGHT TO have, are ENTITLED TO have, and DEMAND to have.

The key words to remember here are "believe," "must," "should," "ought to" and "entitled to." If you think about it carefully *no one*, and *no thing, should, must,* or *ought to* be any way other than the way it is! Stop and think about that statement for a moment because it contains a profound truth. *No one*, and *no thing, should, must,* or *ought to* be any way other than the way it is. Would your life be easier, better and more pleasant if you got everything you thought you *should*? You bet! But is that the real world in which you live? No! In the real world, you may demand that your wife have dinner on the table when you get home from work, but *must* she? No! Would you be happier if she did? Certainly. The important thing to remember is that it is not written anywhere (except in your head!) that others must, or must not, do anything.

> *Dr. Denis, the dentist, came into the examination room to give my teeth one last check. His charming wife Elaine, upon learning that my e-mail address is "noangerdoc," suggested half-playfully that her husband's be changed to "angerdoc." Upon learning of her suggestion, Denis replied, "I can't help it. I'm just a perfectionist. If only everyone in the world were just like me, I wouldn't have any problems!" Elaine and I looked at one another and smiled with our nice clean teeth!*

THE ABC's OF ANGER

Contrary to popular belief, anger does not come "out of the blue." I have had clients describe situations where their anger appeared to come over them so quickly that it seemed almost like a panic attack, seizure or some other form of neurological event. While it may *seem* that way, that's not the way anger works. For all experiences of anger there is a period of time during which the anger builds and, it is during this early stage, that you need to intervene to short circuit the process.

Earlier we discussed the example of tying a shoelace. That illustrated the idea that certain thoughts, because they are overlearned, have become automatic. The same can be said for your anger-producing thoughts. Through years of practice they, too, have become automatic. Changing this automatic process involves breaking down your experience of anger into its various parts, and then exploring the relationship between those parts. In order to do that, you must first learn a new alphabet. In this case, REBT uses the *A,B,C,D,E,F format* to help people understand the origins of their anger and how to better manage it.

According to the A,B,C,D,E,F format:

A = <u>Activator:</u> Activators *trigger*, but *do not cause*, your anger. This is an important distinction to remember. Anyone or anything you come into contact with on a daily basis can serve as an activator for your anger. There are literally millions of potential activators in your life. Another way of thinking about activators is as problems that need to be solved. It is important to recognize and accept that you have *0% control* over the activators in your life.

B = <u>Beliefs:</u> These are what you *think about* the activator. Beliefs can either be helpful or unhelpful for you, others, and for your important relationships. Each of us can think differently about the same activator. Unless you have serious psychological problems, you exercise *100% control* over your beliefs about a particular activator.

Anger-producing beliefs typically include red flag words like "should," "must," and "ought to." When part of your beliefs, these words constitute *demands* made of, and *commands* given to, others. These beliefs tend to be rigid and dogmatic. They are often inflexible. They hinder your efforts at navigating through a world where it is often more helpful to view things in shades of gray, rather than in stark black vs. white terms.

You may conceal your anger-producing beliefs in the form of a question. For example, you are late for an important meeting and a slower car, driven by an older person, is blocking your path. You might angrily ask yourself, "Why do they let old people like that drive?" The anger-producing belief in this case would be, "They *shouldn't* let old people drive!" Another example might involve your boss posting next weeks schedule and changing your hours from days to evenings. You might ask yourself, "Why does he always change my schedule?" Here the anger-producing belief would be, "He *must not* change my schedule!"

C = <u>Consequences:</u> These are the *emotions*, such as anger or irritation, you experience, the *behaviors* you engage in, and the *physical responses* you create for yourself when you hold certain beliefs about the activator. It is important to be as specific as possible when identifying behavioral and physical consequences. Your *behaviors* might include throwing things around the house, cursing at your spouse, and slamming the wall with your fist. *Physical consequences* might include your muscles getting tense, heart racing, blood pressure increasing and hands beginning to shake.

When considering the *emotional consequences* it is helpful to imagine that inside your head is an *Internal Anger Scale*. This scale, represented below, goes from 0, which is no anger, to 10 which represents as intensely angry as you can possibly get. Note that the scale is divided into two ranges, 0-5 and 5-10. The name I have given to the emotion *between 0-5 is irritation*. The name I have given to the emotion *between 5-10 is anger*.

INTERNAL ANGER SCALE

Behavioral Consequences						Physical Consequences
Serious physical agg.	A	10	10	A		Increased blood press.
	N	9	9	N		Increased heart rate
Low-level phys. agg.	G	8	8	G		Rapid, shallow breath.
	E	7	7	E		Increased muscle ten.
Threats/verbal agg.	R	6	6	R		Adrenaline released
		5	5			
Personal Time Out	I	4	4	I		Trembling
	R	3	3	R		
Assertiveness	R.	2	2	R.		Flushed face
		1	1			
		0	0			

As you recall, the goal of managing your anger is to move out of the anger portion of the scale and into the range of the scale associated with irritation. *Why is it important to make the transition from anger to irritation?* First, because the *behaviors* growing out of anger are very different from those growing out of irritation. Second, because the effect of anger on your ability to *solve life's problems* is very different from the effect of irritation on solving the same problems. Third, because the impact of anger on your *parenting skills* and *interpersonal relationships* is much different than the impact on those skills and relationships of being irritated.

As noted earlier, when people first start reading this book they are convinced that other people, or situations they encounter, make them angry. Let's look at an example supplied by a former client who was asked to discuss an incident where he had become angry. Please pay careful attention to the questions I ask "Joe S." during the course of our session because they will help you understand how to complete the "Managing Your Anger" worksheets that play an important role in teaching you how to change anger into irritation.

A SESSION WITH JOE S.

Joe S. was referred for treatment due to anger problems he was having, especially directed towards his wife of eight years. During the first session Joe was introduced to the ABC's of REBT. His homework assignment was to read the first two chapters of this book. In this session we use the ABC format to help him understand a recent angry exchange with his wife.

BPB: "Joe, tell me about the most recent time you got angry."

Joe: "I got real angry at my wife the other night. I came home from work and she had invited that no good, nosey Sheila over to the house! Sheila is nothing but a trouble maker!"

BPB: "What did you *feel* (emotional consequence) when you saw Sheila in the house?"

Joe: "I got real angry. About an 8 on that scale (Internal Anger Scale) I read about."

BPB: "What did you *do* (behavioral consequence) when you saw Sheila in the house?"

Joe: "I screamed at Sheila to leave, and then I pushed my wife into the kitchen and started yelling at her."

BPB: "Finally Joe, what changes did you notice taking place inside your *body* (physical consequences) as you were getting angrier at your wife?"

Joe: "I got to feeling so hot, like I was burning up. My heart started pounding real fast and my muscles were all tense."

Based on this information, you can identify Joe's activator and his three consequences.

Activator: Wife invites Sheila to visit, though Joe has told her not to.

Consequences: His emotional consequence is intense anger (an "8" on the Internal Anger Scale), he pushes his wife into the kitchen and begins yelling at her (behavioral consequences), and his heart rate skyrockets and his muscles become tense (physical consequences).

At this point Joe believes firmly in what is called the *A causes⟶ C Connection*. This is the idea that other people or situations (activators) *make* us angry (emotional consequences).

BPB: "Let me see if I understand this correctly. You are saying that your wife having Sheila over to the house, despite you telling her not to, *made* you angry at the rate of an 8, *made* you push her into the kitchen and start yelling at her, and *made* your muscles tense and got your heart racing. Am I understanding you correctly?"

Joe: "Yeah, that's exactly what I am saying. She *made* me real mad!"

I now invite Joe to look at the relationship he has established in his mind between activators and consequences (*A causes⟶ C Connection*).

BPB: "Joe, let's look at this connection you're making between what your wife did and how you responded. If it were true that your wife *made* you angry in this situation, then *who would be in control of you?*

Joe: "Well, I guess she would be in control of me."

BPB: "What do you think about that? Do you like the idea that she is in control of you? That she is in control of your anger?"

Joe: "No, I don't like that. I want to be in control of myself, but I don't know how to do that."

15

BPB: "I want you to be in control of yourself too. To get in control of yourself we need to look more closely at this idea that your wife caused you to get angry by having Sheila over to the house. This is the idea that activators cause consequences. If that's true, that activators cause consequences, then I want you to continue believing that she made you angry. If it's not true, however, I'm going to ask to give up on believing in that connection. Fair enough?"

Joe: "Okay."

BPB: "Let's imagine that we go to the mall on a Saturday afternoon and pick out one hundred husbands and wives at random. We tell each of the husbands that their wife has invited over to the house a female friend that the husband doesn't like. You get my point? Instead of this situation being between just you and your wife, the same situation occurs, but between one hundred husbands and their wives."

Joe: "Okay, I get it. One hundred husbands and wives."

BPB: "Now Joe, I need you to think *logically* for a moment. You are saying that your wife having Sheila over *made* you angry. If that's true, then how many of the one hundred husbands, upon learning that their wives have had over a woman friend that they disliked, would have to feel angry like you?"

Joe: "Well, I guess most of the husbands would be as angry as I was."

BPB: "Joe, you're not answering my question. You are saying that your wife having Sheila over, the activator in this case, *made* you angry. If that is true then, given the same activator, how many of those one hundred husbands would have to feel like you did--*logically*?"

Joe: "Well, logically they would *all* have to feel the same way I guess."

BPB: "Right. If the activator causes that response in you, logically it should cause the same response in everyone encountering it. Now, I want you to tell me *how likely* it would be that all one hundred husbands would experience the same reaction you did?

Joe: "Geeze, I don't know. But it would be a lot I can tell you that."

16

BPB: "Maybe fifty husbands? Maybe seventy-five? Let's assume that ninety-nine out of the one hundred husbands had the same reaction you did. Even if ninety-nine out of the one hundred husbands experienced the same reaction you did, that means *one did not*. And if even one husband does not experience the same response you did, what does that mean about the activator causing the consequences? Is that relationship true or false?"

Joe: "Well, when you look at it that way, it's false."

BPB: "Exactly! So do activator's cause your anger?"

Joe: "I guess not."

BPB: "Does your wife *make* you mad when she invites Sheila over?"

Joe: "No."

BPB: "Right. She doesn't make you mad. And if she doesn't make you mad, then who does?"

Joe: "I guess I do."

BPB: "Another way of looking at this situation involves asking yourself *how much control* you have over what has happened. On a scale going from 0%, which is none, to 100%, which is complete or total, how much control do you have over your wife inviting Sheila over?"

Joe: "I don't have any control over my wife. If I did, she wouldn't invite Sheila over."

BPB: "Right. But now the question becomes, 'How much control do you have over *how you think* about your wife inviting Sheila over?' "

Joe: "Well, like you've been teaching me, I have total control over how I think about things."

BPB: "That's right Joe. So which is going to be a better use of your time? Trying to change your wife, over whom you have no control, or trying to change your thoughts about what your wife does, over which you have total control?"

Joe: "Since I have all the control over my thoughts, I guess I need to *stop blaming* Sheila for my anger and start working on changing my thinking, Doc."

BPB: "We all need to work on our own thinking, Joe. Welcome to the human race!"

Once Joe has broken the *A causes→C Connection* (i.e., the idea that other people or situations *cause* his anger), we move on to identify his anger-producing beliefs.

BPB: "Joe, do you remember what you *thought* when you saw Sheila over visiting? What did you tell yourself? What went through your head?"

Joe: "I remember thinking 'Sheila *should* get out of my house! I've told my wife a million times to keep her away from us; she *should* do what I tell her to do! I don't go against my wife's wishes, so she *shouldn't* go against mine!' "

Here we see Joe, as Albert Ellis describes it, "shoulding-on" his wife.

BPB: "Joe, it sounds like you have some pretty strong beliefs about what your wife should and shouldn't do. What are those "red flag" words we discussed before that cause your anger?"

Joe: "I know Doc, the shoulds, musts and oughts. There they are again!"

BPB: "Joe, when you don't get what you demand of your wife, or when she doesn't do what you think she should, how do you feel?"

Joe: "I make myself angry big time!"

Joe can now make the connection between his *demanding/commanding* beliefs and the production of his anger. Once this connection is clear Joe needs help converting his anger into irritation. That is accomplished by guiding him through the *D, E,* and *F* parts of this process.

D = <u>Disputation</u>: This is just a fancy way of saying that you need to *argue against* your anger-producing beliefs. Disputing anger-producing beliefs is the most difficult part of the anger management process because, as noted earlier, you think anger helps you control other people, it's overlearned, and it makes you feel powerful. Also, questioning the way you have always thought about the activators in your life takes *considerable courage* and the ability to ask yourself tough questions like the ones I now ask Joe to consider.

BPB: "Joe, since we agree that it is your thinking about your wife having Sheila over that makes you angry, we need to help you find a new way of thinking. Part of that involves having you look at your anger-producing beliefs to see whether or not they are true in the *real* world, or are part of some *fantasy* world. One question you can ask yourself about your anger-producing beliefs is, 'Where is it written...?' In this case, 'Where is it written that that your wife *must* do as you tell her regarding Sheila?' or 'Where is written that, simply because you don't go against her wishes, she *must not* go against yours?' "

Joe: "Well, I guess its not written anywhere."

BPB: "I would disagree with that. These beliefs appear to be written in bold letters in at least one place. Where is that?"

Joe: "You mean in my head?"

BPB: "Exactly! Just because they are written in your head, does that make them true?"

Joe: "I guess not."

BPB: "Another question you could ask yourself is, 'Do these beliefs help me or hurt me?' "

Joe: "Thinking this way hurts me. It makes me angry, causes me to push my wife, and sends my heart rate through the roof."

BPB: "Another disputation question is, 'Do these beliefs help my important relationships, in this case with my wife, or do they hurt that relationship?' "

Joe: "Thinking this way hurts my relationship with my wife. She is afraid of me now. She never knows when I am going to blow up or what it will be over."

BPB: "Do these beliefs solve the problem of your wife inviting Sheila over to the house?

19

Joe: "No, they just make the problem worse by making it more difficult for my wife and me to talk about it."

BPB: "The last question you could ask yourself is, 'Do I always do what others tell me to do?' "

Joe: "No, I guess not. Actually, when someone *tells* me to do something, I usually do the exact opposite. Maybe that's what my wife is doing? I need to accept that she is free to make her own choices, even ones I don't like, and that I can't control her."

E = Effective Beliefs: Once Joe has successfully disputed his anger-producing beliefs, using the types of questions asked of him above, he needs to replace them with beliefs resulting in irritation. For Joe to replace his anger-producing beliefs in this situation with beliefs resulting in happiness, for example, would be unrealistic. When we don't get what we want from life or from others, it would be crazy to be *happy* about that outcome. There is, however, an emotional response between anger and happiness available to Joe in this situation. That response, as you will recall, is irritation.

As noted earlier, anger-producing beliefs are *commanding and demanding* in nature and include words like *should* and *must*. Effective beliefs are what REBT refers to as "*preferential beliefs.*" That is, they are beliefs of preference, and include words like *wishing, hoping, desiring, preferring* and *wanting*. These beliefs recognize that you have *0% control* over the activator. In this case, Joe's effective belief would sound like this:

Joe: "I would *prefer* that my wife not have Sheila over to the house, but I have *no control* over what she decides to do."

F = New Feelings: Here you re-rate the original consequences (emotional, behavioral and physical) after substituting your effective beliefs for your anger-producing beliefs.

BPB: "Joe, let's imagine that when you saw Sheila over at the house, rather than thinking, 'I've told my wife a million times to keep Sheila away from us, she *should* do what I tell her to do!' or 'I don't go against her wishes, so she *shouldn't* go against mine!' you thought, 'I would prefer that my wife not have Sheila over to the house, but I have *no control* over what she decides to do.' Based on that new effective belief, what would happen to your anger? Would it go up, stay the same, or go down?

Joe: "It would go down to about a 3 or 4 on that scale. I still wouldn't be happy about it, but I wouldn't be so angry about it either."

BPB: "We wouldn't expect you to be happy about it. But there is a feeling between anger and happiness in this case. Do you remember what we are calling that feeling?"

Joe: "Yeah, that's the irritation stuff we talked about."

BPB: "Right. Remember that we want you to go from being angry in this situation to being irritated. And we want you to do that because, well, why don't you tell me?"

Joe: "Because if I am irritated, and not angry, chances are I would not push her around, my body wouldn't get all messed up, and I would probably be better at solving this problem I'm having with her."

BPB: "That's right Joe. Now you get it!"

One of the points I emphasize with clients, as they compare their anger-producing beliefs to their effective beliefs, is how the latter are true while the former are false.

BPB: "Joe, I want to ask you one last thing. Which of your two beliefs is true in the real world? That your wife must not have Sheila over to the house, or that you wish she wouldn't have Sheila over to the house but you have no control over what she does?"

Joe: "The second belief is true."

BPB: "Isn't it interesting how, when we tell ourselves lies, we get ourselves angry and all worked up and when we tell ourselves things we know are true, the anger goes away."

Joe: "You're right Doc, I've been telling myself lies for a long time."

Joe and I systematically dissected his anger using one of the "Managing Your Anger" worksheets found in the Appendix. Using these forms to work through specific situations where you have become angry reinforces the idea that you create your own anger based on how you think. You also remind yourself that, by changing your thinking, you can eliminate anger and replace it with more helpful irritation. The more you *practice* using these forms, the sooner new ways of thinking will replace the old, automatic ways of thinking that produced anger.

You now have what I consider to be the most important tool necessary for constructing a life with significantly less anger. We will review other tools in a later chapter. Whether or not you pick up any of these tools, and use them to improve your life, is completely up to you!

SUGGESTED HOMEWORK:

A.)   Complete one "Managing Your Anger" form as found in the Appendix. A completed example of this form, based on the "Session with Joe S." covered in this chapter, is supplied. You may make copies of the blank forms as needed in order to complete future assignments. Remember that disputing your anger-producing beliefs will be the most difficult part of the exercise so you may want to re-read that portion of the chapter.

B.)   True/False: Activators cause consequences.

C.)   According to REBT, "It is not life's circumstances that make you angry. Rather, it is how you _____ to _____ about those circumstances that causes your anger."

D.)   Which three "red flag" words are related to the creation of anger?
       1.)_____ 2.)_____ 3.)_____

E.)   Effective beliefs differ from anger-producing beliefs in that effective beliefs are_____, while anger-producing beliefs are _____ and _____.

F.)   While we have ____% control over the activators in our lives, we do have _____% control over how we _____about the activators.

G.)   According to the Internal Anger Scale, 0-5 is associated with _____, while 5-10 is associated with _____.

H.)   _____your anger-producing beliefs will be the most difficult part of the A,B,C,D,E, F process.

CHAPTER THREE

THE MANY FACES OF ANGER

Entitlement

Anger has many faces. For some, anger is the result of the mistaken belief that they are *entitled* to certain things from others or from life generally.

> *For many years a keen sense of entitlement underpinned much of my anger. Born into an affluent family due to the hard work of my father, I believed myself entitled to the "good life" he provided for my mother, brother and myself. When life refused my demand for a high paying job (I was too smart to waste my time finishing college!), I angered myself greatly. How dare the world refuse me what I was entitled to! To this day I recall my mother saying, "You know Brad, you've got to get over this idea that the world owes you a living!" How right she was.*

To believe that you are entitled to something means that it is "due," or "owed to," you—oftentimes without you having done anything to earn it. Some entitlement related beliefs include:

--"I'm entitled to be treated fairly at all times."

--"I'm entitled to have a good paying job."

--"I'm entitled to be taken care of by others." (including friends, spouses, family, the government, etc.)

--"I'm entitled to have what I want, when I want it, without expending any effort or experiencing any discomfort."

When you *believe* you are entitled to something, and don't get it, you make yourself very angry. When one reflects on the whole notion of entitlement, however, one is immediately struck by the reality that *no one is entitled to anything*! The following stories illustrate my point.

One group member comes immediately to mind when I think of entitlement related anger. Shelly, a former nurse in the Marines, cared for sick and dying children at a local hospital. As a result of her many good works she believed her own family to be immune from the profound sadness she encountered on a daily basis. She entered an anger management group not long after her ten-year-old son had been diagnosed with leukemia. In addition to her anger at the court for ordering her to attend my program (over a disagreement she allegedly had with her husband), she was even more profoundly angry over the fact that her own child had become ill. It quickly became apparent that her beliefs included, among others: "I've helped all these other children and their families over the years so these things *shouldn't* happen to my family. I am *entitled* to a life free of pain because of all I've done to help others." Delicately, I worked on getting her to at least look at how her beliefs were contributing to her anger, but she was not ready to let go of them just yet. As a matter of fact, she stormed out of the first session and I was convinced that she wouldn't return. And she didn't--until three weeks later. At the outset of the group she graciously apologized for her behavior and said, "You know, you were right about why I was so angry that first session. I mean, I know all about that 'bad things happen to good people' stuff, it's just that I couldn't believe that this was happening to *me*. I guess we all think we are special somehow; that we won't have to go through what other people go through. You know, since I figured this all out in my head, I spend a lot less energy being angry, and a lot more time being grateful for those moments my son and I have left."

Another example of entitlement related anger I've never forgotten centered on the experiences of figure skater Nancy Kerrigan. As you recall, Nancy was scheduled to compete for a place on the U.S. Olympic Figure Skating team when she was attacked by an assailant we later learned had been hired by her main competitor, Tonya Harding. That particular week's issue of either *Time* or *Newsweek* ran a picture of Ms. Kerrigan on the front, grimacing in pain, under the caption "Why?" Ms. Kerrigan seemed to be asking the question, "Why did this happen to me?" which, transformed into a statement, really sounds like the anger-producing belief, "This *shouldn't* have happened to me!" Had Ms. Kerrigan been my client, and had she discussed with me her anger over this event, my first question to her would have been, "Nancy, can you give me one reason why this *shouldn't* have happened to you? Why you are so special that you are *entitled* to avoid the bad things that happen to the rest of us?" I've always assumed (during this fictional exchange!) that, as she pondered my questions, her anger would lessen as she realized that she was neither so special, nor entitled, to avoid the travails each of us experiences at some point in our lives.

> *Occasionally my sense of entitlement gets the best of me. No where is that more likely to occur than when I am stuck in traffic. To lessen my anger I use the following technique: I begin screaming out my entitlement related beliefs. "Don't these people know who I am? They should just get out of my way! Don't they know I have people to heal?" As I really get involved in my tirade, arms flailing wildly, a smile crosses my lips followed by a hearty laugh. One of the best ways to deal with anger-producing beliefs is by exposing them for all to hear. In almost all cases they are both ridiculous and hilarious!*

24

Control

Another face adopted by anger is that of control. Almost by definition, *anger is about trying to control other people.* When others don't do what we think they *should*, we make ourselves angry. Earlier we noted that anger is difficult to treat because some people believe that anger works by getting them what they demand. As they get angrier, and people give in to their demands, the angry person concludes that it was their anger that *made* the other person do their bidding.

There are at least three problems with believing that your anger is capable of controlling others. First, it overlooks the fact that others have *freedom of choice,* and that their compliance with your demand is not because you *made* them do anything but, rather, it represents a *decision to comply* on their part. Second, simply because someone chooses to give in to your angry demands today does not preclude you from having problems with them again in the future. For example, a child may give in to your demand that he complete his homework in the present, all the while plotting how he will repay your efforts at controlling him in the future. Especially in those cases where individuals perceive that they have less power than the individual making demands of them, they will comply outwardly all the while seething inside as they wait for an opportunity to even the score.

> *Children understand keenly that they are not as powerful as adults are and often go underground with their anger. I recall one adolescent client telling me how his father had been angry with him for years, always trying to control his behavior at home and at school. One day his father told him to mail an important tax related document that needed to be postmarked by a certain date. My client agreed, then "accidentally on purpose" forgot, resulting in his father incurring a sizable tax penalty. The moral of the story is that, when you try to control others, you eventually learn that "what goes around, comes around."*

Third, when others perceive that we are trying to control them, *they often do the exact opposite of what we are demanding and commanding of them.* The relationship between control, and resistance to control, is made more vivid in my mind by recalling the spaceship Enterprise from the old *Star Trek* television series. The ship possessed a number of "rays" and "beams" designed to protect it from enemy attack. One such beam was called the "tractor beam." This beam was designed to lock on to an object in space and pull it towards the ship. That is, the beam was designed to *control* that object. Even if you've never seen an episode of *Star Trek,* I bet you can guess what the object tries doing once the tractor beam is locked on. Exactly! It does everything in its power to resist that beam and break free from it. In many respects your anger is like that beam. When another person perceives that you have locked on to them with your "anger beam" they resist your efforts at control and try furiously to move away from you. Learning to manage your anger is about learning how to turn that beam off!

Ultimately, the belief that you can control another human being is a myth—albeit a myth shared by many. By definition, a myth is "a fiction or half-truth that forms part of an ideology." In this case, it forms a personal ideology or way of seeing others and the world. The truth about control is that, beyond your own thoughts, feelings and behaviors, *you can control no one or no thing.* For many, steeped in a culture like our own that believes we can and must control every one and every thing, this is a very bitter pill to swallow. Swallow it you must, however, if you are ever going to master your anger.

The next time you are at the beach, bend over and grab a handful of sand. As you squeeze the sand more tightly, what happens to it? It gradually seeps between your fingers. As you try controlling another with your anger, what happens to your relationship with him or her? It, too, pours through your fingers and is lost.

Fantasy

Anger frequently adopts the face of *fantasy*. Here we introduce the notion of anger as a product of living in the "World of Should." In addition to the *real world* in which you live--the "World of Is"--there is another world where things are as you *think* they should, must, and ought to be. This is the "World of Should."

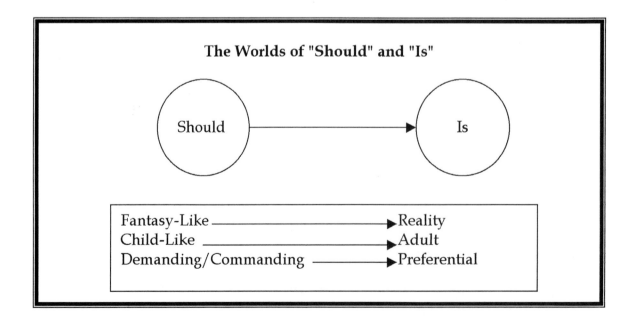

26

In the "World of Should," things are perfect. They are perfect, not surprisingly, because they are exactly the way *you think* they should, must, and ought to be! Life is fair in the "World of Should" (at least according to *your* definition of fairness). You always get what you want, when you want it, without delay or interference from others. You treat bosses, children, spouses and others well, and they respond in kind. Hard work is always rewarded. People never lie or gossip about you. The "system" gets the "bad people," and never involves "good folks" like you. Parents love and support their children, and children love and obey their parents. On and on it goes! What a wonderful place the "World of Should" would be, if only it weren't a fantasy existing exclusively in your mind!

The "World of Is," as you would expect, differs greatly from the "World of Should." The "World of Is" is the so-called "real world," where you *really* live. In the "World of Is" you treat people well, but they don't always treat you well. In the "World of Is" life is not always fair. When clients referred by the court call to enroll in an anger management class they sometimes upset themselves over being treated unfairly by "the system." When I ask how old they are, and inquire further as to whether or not they are only now (at the ripe old age of 30 for example!) learning that the world is often unfair, they quickly calm themselves down. In the "World of Is" you work hard and wait for what you want, instead of getting it immediately. Sometimes you are compelled to accept the fact that you won't get what you want, no matter how long you have waited or how hard you have worked. In the "World of Is" there are times when "bad things happen to good people."

One of your tasks while reading this book is to find a way to spend less time living in the "World of Should," and more time living in the "World of Is." The "World of Is" is where *adults* live. The "World of Should," not surprisingly, is where *children* live. Those of you who are parents will surely agree with this observation. A child "pitching a fit" is really no different than an adult angering him or her self. Aren't both really demanding that they get their way? Aren't both really insisting that the world give them what they believe they should, must, and ought to have?

Shame

Shame is one of the seven emotions researchers have identified as common to all human beings. Most agree that shame is the result of a strong sense of guilt, embarrassment or disgrace. Like anger, it can be a very powerful emotional experience. Unlike anger, however, appropriate amounts of shame can be beneficial since the goal of shame is to help the individual experiencing it correct his or her behavior so that the behavior is no longer contrary to their core values.

Some authors contend that anger is a product of shame. While I find their arguments unpersuasive, there does appear to be an important connection between anger and shame for some people. The connection is to be found in the fact that shame is an emotion that accompanies being "dis-covered." Shame is what we feel when our inappropriate behavior is uncovered and made available for all to see. It is the emotion we experience when we are laid bare psychologically as the world passes judgment on the choices we have made.

For some, the prospect of experiencing shame is psychologically overwhelming. They cannot tolerate being "dis-covered." They cannot bear looking at themselves openly and honestly which, of course, shame requires of us. Rather than experience shame, these individuals transform that emotional experience into anger. Their anger, often directed towards those who have discovered them, allows them to feel powerful and potent again, where once their shame had made them feel powerless. Their anger allows them to point fingers at, and blame, the very people who brought their transgressions to light. While getting angry has all these supposed advantages attached to it, it also postpones the learning process for these individuals as they focus on accusing and blaming others, all the while neglecting to evaluate and correct their own behavior. Experience teaches me that this strategy of converting shame into anger may work in the short term, but seldom does "life" allow it work over the long haul. At some point, the shamed person will have to learn his or her lesson.

The politician had been exposed. Wagging his finger and staring defiantly into the television camera, he angrily proclaimed his innocence and stated that he had never had "sexual relations" with the young woman in question. Shame converted into anger? You decide.

SOME FINAL THOUGHTS ON ANGER

People oftentimes ask whether anger is a greater problem today than it has been in the past. My answer to that question is "Yes." Consider that simply looking at the past decade, from the 1980's to the 1990's, cases of reported domestic abuse jumped over 100%. Experts estimate that incidents involving road rage increase at a rate of about 7% per year. The most devastating violent crimes to occur in schools in the history of our country have occurred in the last two years. From increasing rates of violent crime, to domestic violence, to road rage, to children killing children in schoolyards, the evidence is all around us. But why are we angrier today?

We are angrier because we are currently living through what I refer to as the *Age of Entitlement*. By this I mean that we are living during a moment in history when almost everyone believes that he or she is entitled to, or owed, every resource society has to offer without doing anything to earn those resources. From free housing to a free education, from free medical care to subsidized incomes, this march towards declaring almost everything in our culture an "entitlement" is grounded in the political and social changes that have shaped our country over the last forty years. While no doubt well intentioned, those who have pressed for expanding the notion of what constitutes an entitlement had no idea that what they were really creating is a breeding ground for much of the anger and resentment we see around us today. Just as a fire needs oxygen in order to burn so, too, does anger need incendiary beliefs, including anger-producing beliefs regarding entitlement, to continue burning.

In addition to fueling much of the anger around us, this pervasive sense of entitlement robs us of one of life's most noble and uplifting experiences--the ability to experience *gratitude*. Gratitude is the state of being grateful or thankful for some one or some thing in your life. Think about it for a moment. When you believe that you are entitled to some thing, and do not get it, you make yourself very angry indeed. When you believe that you are entitled to some thing, and you receive that which you believe you are entitled to, there is no joy or gratitude because, after all, it is simply your due. Recognizing that *you are not entitled to anything* douses the flames of anger and reopens a pathway to experiencing gratitude.

> *In my adopted hometown of Memphis a local country-western radio station interviewed me on the topic of anger for its lively 5:00 am Sunday morning public service program. The station call letters sounding something like "Froggy," they naturally referred to their on air personalities by such catchy names as "Polly Wog," "Danger Frog," etc. On this particular day Ms. Wog was interviewing me. At the end of our twenty-three minutes together Polly asked, "Dr. Barris, what is the opposite of anger?" From somewhere, I still don't know where, I replied, "The opposite of anger is gratitude." While that may or may not be true, it still strikes me as being a pretty good place to start looking for anger's opposite.*

If gratitude is a potential antidote to anger, then so, too, is humor. Anger, as you now know, is the product of your faulty thinking. Humor is also a product of how you perceive, or think about, certain things. As you saw in the vignette where I described how I dealt with my anger while stuck in a traffic jam, our anger-producing beliefs are often humorous and ridiculous in the extreme. Developing an appreciation for the absurdity and laughable nature of your unhelpful thinking will lead to less anger in your life.

Throughout this book you are learning that, whatever face anger assumes, *it always involves a choice*. You never hear me say, "I was driving to work this morning and a guy cut me off. That really made me angry!" Were I to say that it would imply that, given that situation, I had no choice but to get angry. As we have seen, however, it is not the activator (being cut off) that makes me angry, but rather how I think about that activator. Periodically (but much less often than before I learned these techniques!) I will remark, "This guy cut me off on the way in to the office today and I *chose to anger myself* about it!" By phrasing it that way I remind myself of the fact that I always have a *choice* regarding whether or not I get angry in any situation.

A colleague of mine, Dr. Ed Nottingham, helps his clients think about the relationship between an activator and their anger by having them imagine the activator handing the client an "invitation" to anger him or her self. Think about it like you would an invitation to a party. Most invitations list the nature of the party, it's location and time, and end with "Please RSVP." The RSVP requests that the recipient respond either by accepting or declining the invitation. Our response to anger works in much the same way. When the activator either does something you think he or she *shouldn't* have, or doesn't do something you think he or she *should* have, they are really just sending you an invitation to anger yourself. Given that it is always *your choice* whether or not to accept the invitation, I would strongly recommend a polite "No thanks!" The choice to anger yourself or not, in any given situation, is always yours.

By using the A,B,C,D,E,F technique for controlling anger you will never get angry again, right? *Wrong!* Chances are excellent that you will accept future invitations from life to anger yourself. Using this technique, however, means that you will accept far fewer of those invitations and, of those you do accept, you will anger yourself less intensely and for shorter periods of time.

No one is born angry. *You were not born angry!* It has taken you years to *learn* how to make yourself angry. Changing anger into irritation, using the ABC's of REBT, requires *constant self-awareness* and *practice!* The more you practice these techniques, the more they become second nature. What were once automatic thoughts that produced anger become, instead, automatic thoughts producing irritation. Where once you engaged in self-defeating behaviors growing out of your anger, you now find yourself motivated to solve the various problems life throws your way. Yes, it is hard to do. And even more emphatically "Yes!" it is worth doing.

> *During my seminars someone always makes the observation that, while using the ABC's makes great sense, it appears difficult to do in practice. At which point I state, "You know, you're right. This technique looks straightforward, but it's not easy to do--at least initially. But now I have a question for you. Do you still poop in your pants?" A question met with surprise and then laughter. "I suspect that you don't. Was it difficult, when you were two years-old, learning how not to poop in your pants? Probably. That just tells me that you have done something in your life that was difficult to accomplish. You can do the same thing with your anger!"*

SUGGESTED HOMEWORK:

A.)   Complete one "Managing Your Anger" form as found in the Appendix.

B.)   List the various "faces" worn by anger.

        1.)_____

        2.)_____

        3.)_____

        4.)_____

C.)   The World of _____ is where adults live. The World of _____ is where children, and angry adults, spend most of their time.

D.)   When you attempt to control others by using anger, they_____
_____.

E.)   In the Appendix you will find a worksheet entitled "Cost-Benefit Analysis." An example of how to complete this exercise is included. Conduct a Cost-Benefit Analysis the next time you anger yourself. The goal is to determine whether or not your anger helped achieve your *long-term goals in a particular situation*. The achievement of short-term goals is not considered as important as achieving longer-term goals.

F.)   A sense of entitlement robs you of the ability to experience
_____.

G.)   True/False: You were born angry.

CHAPTER FOUR

STOCKING YOUR PSYCHOLOGICAL TOOLBOX: ADDITIONAL TECHNIQUES FOR MANAGING ANGER

To this point you have learned that managing anger involves disputing your anger-producing beliefs and replacing them, instead, with preferential beliefs resulting in irritation. Is disputing anger-producing beliefs the only way to lessen your anger? The answer is "No." Is it potentially the most profound and long lasting way to manage anger? The answer to that question is a resounding "Yes!"

What do I mean by profound and long lasting change? I mean that once you abandon beliefs that you are entitled to various things from life; or that you can control other people; or that the world and others should, must, and ought to be a certain way, your entire "philosophy of life" changes. Once you make these changes in your worldview anger becomes, in large part, a feature of your past. Challenging your anger-producing beliefs, and replacing them with more preferential beliefs emphasizing your lack of control over the activator represents, from my perspective, the "ideal" way to manage anger.

In the real world, however, not everyone is capable of using this ideal form of anger management, nor does everyone want to expend the time and effort necessary to critically examine, abandon, and then replace their anger-producing beliefs. Just as a craftsperson needs more than one tool in order to practice his or her trade so, too, do you need more than one tool in order to help you manage anger. Reviewing the nature of those other tools, and how best to use them, is where we turn next.

MANAGING POTENTIAL STRESSORS

We live in a world where everyone, it seems, is trying to rid him or her self of stress. Self-help programs and books are written to address the problem of stress. Vitamins and various foods are touted as relievers of stress. Stress management talks are the number one requested presentations made by psychologist types like myself to businesses and their employees. If your goal is the complete elimination of stress, I have the same bad news for you that I had regarding the complete elimination of anger. It simply can't be done.

Stress is an inevitable part of life and, even if you could completely rid yourself of it, chances are good that you wouldn't want to. An appropriate level of stress is what motivates you to perform at home, school and work in ways you never thought possible. Great athletes are constantly striving to find "the zone" which represents an optimal level of stress that leads, in turn, to optimal performance on the track, field or court. Stress, viewed from this perspective, is a positive force in your life. If appropriate levels of stress improve performance, than too low or too high levels of stress interfere with performance. Finding the correct balance is the goal of stress management.

Where does stress come from? It is in answering this question that most people make the same mistake that they make when answering the question, "But why do I get so angry?" Just as you *used* to believe that other people or situations made you angry so, too, do most people (perhaps including yourself!) believe that certain things external to them create their stress. Things that they believe create high levels of stress include illnesses (either personal or within the family), financial problems, work related problem and relationship problems at home. As you have learned regarding anger, however, things external to you carry no meaning other than the meaning you *choose* to give to them. Some meanings (beliefs) result in destructively high levels of stress, while other meanings result in helpful levels of stress.

When you assign meanings to events that result in the production of high levels of stress, you are also making yourself more vulnerable to responding angrily to the various activators in your life. Think of it this way. Under stress, the threshold at which you will choose to anger yourself over a given activator is lowered. This means that an activator you could easily handle when not under high levels of stress all of a sudden becomes an activator that you anger yourself over when experiencing high levels of stress. To the extent that you can manage your beliefs regarding potentially stressful aspects of your life, you raise the anger threshold and reduce the likelihood of making yourself angry.

Tools for Managing Anger

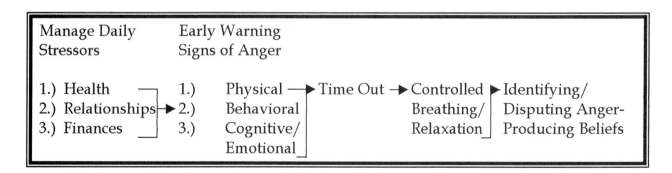

33

YOUR BODY AND ANGER: A BRIEF OWNER'S MANUAL

Unfortunately, none of us receives an owner's manual for the most complex device we will ever operate--our own body. Were we given such a manual at birth panic attacks, and other strange bodily experiences, would be much less threatening. If we fully understood how our body's worked anger might also be more easily managed.

Most people, professional therapists included, lack an appreciation for the fact that the systems our bodies turn "on" when we experience anxiety are the same ones turned "on" during anger. Since this is the case, it is possible to use some of the same techniques for turning anger "off" that have been developed for lessen anxiety. David Barlow, Ph.D. and Michelle Craske, Ph.D., in their state of the art manual <u>Mastery of Your Anxiety and Panic II</u>, provide the clearest description yet of how these anxiety/anger producing systems work.

The fight or flight system is "hard-wired," or genetically part of each of us. Researchers suggest that this system became part of our makeup through the evolutionary process of natural selection. Back in the days when men and women lived in caves, and fought with each other and with wild beasts, the fight or flight system was necessary for survival. When confronted with danger, our bodies evolved in such a way that certain responses kicked in quickly, thereby allowing us to take immediate action. Overall, the purpose of the fight or flight system is to prepare us, in the face of a threat, to either flee that threat, or stand and fight against it. As Barlow and Craske point out, "the purpose of the system is to protect the organism."

The Physiology of Anger

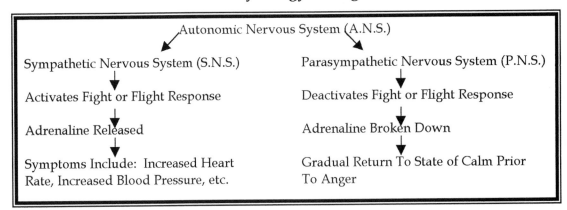

Autonomic Nervous System (A.N.S.)

Sympathetic Nervous System (S.N.S.) → Parasympathetic Nervous System (P.N.S.)

Activates Fight or Flight Response → Deactivates Fight or Flight Response

Adrenaline Released → Adrenaline Broken Down

Symptoms Include: Increased Heart Rate, Increased Blood Pressure, etc. → Gradual Return To State of Calm Prior To Anger

When we perceive a threat, messages are relayed from our brain to a branch of our nervous system called the Autonomic Nervous System (ANS). The ANS is further subdivided into the Sympathetic Nervous System (SNS) and the Parasympathetic Nervous System (PNS). These two systems work together to either activate or deactivate the fight or flight system. When the SNS is activated certain chemicals, e.g., adrenaline and noradrenaline, are released from the adrenal glands in the kidneys. These chemicals get us "pumped up" and ready for action, whatever that action might be.

The SNS responds very quickly to perceived threats and typically works on an "all-or-none" basis. One way to think about the SNS is like a light switch that is either completely "on" or "off." In other words, when it is activated, all of the accompanying physiological changes take place. People who get angry notice changes in their arms, shoulders, faces, legs and toes. The SNS literally arouses the entire body in the presence of some form of threat.

Understanding the physiology of anger has important implications for managing anger. First, when you make yourself angry, you activate the SNS. With that activation comes the symptoms people reliably experience and record in their "Managing Your Anger" forms under the heading of "Physical Consequences". Those symptoms include rapid heart rate, increased blood pressure, rapid, shallow breathing, increased muscle tension and sweating. Second, with the passage of time, other chemicals will break down the adrenaline in your system and the PSN will intervene to help calm you down. This process, however, can take an extended period of time depending on the individual. Third, there are things you can do, while waiting for the PNS to intervene, to calm yourself more quickly. Two strategies, discussed below, show you how to calm yourself either by removing yourself from the presence of a specific activator, or by using various relaxation strategies while still remaining in contact with the activator.

TAKING A PERSONAL TIME OUT (PTO)

Most adults, especially those with children, have either heard of, or used, the behavior management technique known as *time out*. When used with children, this technique is designed to help the child regain control of him or her self by removing him or her from an environment that may be reinforcing what their caregiver considers to be inappropriate behavior. For some children, time out can be an effective way of getting them to alter their behavior.

Why, then, would I be proposing a Personal Time Out (PTO) for adults? If you've been following along closely, the answer should be obvious. As you recall in our discussion of the "World of Should" and the "World of Is," the former is the world children live in, while the latter is where adults live. When you anger yourself, when you live in the "World of Should," you essentially *regress to a child-like state!* Pitching a fit, throwing a temper tantrum, you name it. If anger is associated with thinking and behaving like a child, then being able to give *yourself* a PTO makes perfect sense.

When instructing his clients on how to take a PTO a colleague, Dr. Tom Kirchberg, describes the following procedure:

"Most of us are familiar with the use of a Time Out during sports events. We can probably remember some game when our favorite team just couldn't get it together and we were sitting there in front of the TV shouting at the coach, 'Call a time out! Call a time out!' In a ballgame the coach calls a time out when the players begin to get rattled and are not performing well. The coach calls a time out in order to help the players cool down, regroup, and get back into the game in a winning way. In a similar way, a PTO can provide you with an opportunity to get your act together. It is particularly useful when you find yourself becoming progressively more angry. Using a PTO gives you another opportunity to be responsible for yourself, to take control of your own behavior, and to handle anger in more productive ways. When you choose a PTO for yourself, you reinforce the notion that you are your own 'coach,' and the one in control of your anger."

As we have seen, using REBT to manage anger is a skill that can be learned and that needs to be practiced daily. The same is true when using a PTO. Successful use of a PTO involves the following steps:

STEP 1.)   Recognize the *early warning signs* of anger. As with all warning signs, these are designed to protect you from danger. In this case, the dangers are associated with becoming angry. Warning signs include:

> --*Physical warning signs:* increased blood pressure, increased heart rate, sweating, shaking, dizziness
>
> --*Behavioral warning signs:* throwing things, hitting things or people, yelling
>
> --*Cognitive/emotional warning signs:* where you find yourself becoming increasingly angry as you think to yourself "She *shouldn't* have done that!" or "I've helped him in the past, so he *should* help me now!"

Use these warning signs as "red flags" for your anger and as "cues" to take a PTO.

Over the years I have trained myself to recognize a particular physical response that warns me of my increasing anger. Whenever my left hand begins shaking, I know it's time for me to take a PTO. Cueing in on that simple signal has saved me a lot of trouble over the years!

STEP 2.)   Upon noticing one or more of the above warning signs, tell the activator that *you are angering yourself* and will need to leave for a period of time. At least one hour, possibly more, depending on how angry you have made yourself. Don't be afraid to ask for more time if you think you need it.

STEP 3.)   Assure the activator that, after calming yourself down, you *will return* to work on whatever the problem is between the two of you. Remember that taking a time out also requires that you take a "time in."

STEP 4.)   If the activator reacts negatively to your request for time to calm yourself down, you can remind him or her that you are trying to regain control of yourself so you can deal with them more reasonably. If they are familiar with REBT, you might *lovingly* remind them that they are upsetting themselves over your request, and may need to take a PTO themselves!

STEP 5.)   Pat yourself on the back! If you take a PTO and regain control of yourself, rather than saying and/or doing something that hurts you or others as you would have in the past, pat yourself on the back psychologically for dealing better with your anger. One popular definition of insanity is "doing the same things over and over again with the expectation of a different outcome." By taking a PTO, you break the old pattern of doing things and can look forward to less anger and a different, more favorable outcome for all involved.

One final point about PTO's. No athlete would go into a contest without first formulating a plan, and then practicing that plan before the game. In the same way it is important for you to *practice taking a PTO* before you really need to use it. You may choose to practice taking a PTO during a situation where you reliably become *irritated* so you will know how to respond should you become angry. By practicing this skill beforehand, it will be available when you need it most.

It is clear to me that men do not have a monopoly on anger or aggressive behavior. In our anger management groups men frequently report trying to "get away" from their partners in order to "cool down," only to have their efforts resisted by partners who become even angrier and attempt to block their departure. The most common reason given by women for resisting their partner's efforts to leave is that "if he leaves, we'll never talk about our problems." If your partner asks for a time out, it is crucial that you allow him or her to leave so they can regain control of themselves. It is also important that the partner who is leaving promise to return, at some point in the future, so the problem can be discussed and hopefully resolved.

RELAXATION STRATEGIES

As you now know, anger activates the fight or flight system in your body. This results in tense muscles, quicker breaths, increased blood pressure, and a heightened pulse rate. Shallow, rapid breaths can cause further activation of the SNS. One way to turn the system "off" is to calm this physiological reaction by systematically relaxing the body. Edmund Jacobson, a psychologist, physician and physiologist conducted a series of studies in the 1920's and 1930's. He applied techniques of relaxation to anxiety, insomnia, tics, headaches and depression. Jacobson suggested that just as the mind can influence the body (your automatic thoughts can cause physiological arousal), so too can the body have an impact on the mind (relaxing your body can also lead to more relaxing, soothing thoughts). Instead of changing your thoughts, which would change your level of physiological arousal, Jacobson suggested that relaxation techniques indirectly affected the way individuals think. Thus, when you are getting angry, you can look at your anger-producing beliefs, or you can attempt to relax your body, which will then help alter your thinking.

A prominent psychologist, Jerry Deffenbacher, Ph.D., has conducted numerous studies with individuals who experience dramatic amounts of anger. The results of these studies confirm Jacobson's hypothesis. When angry people are taught some basic relaxation procedures they are able to manage their anger much more effectively.

Learning to use relaxation strategies is not a complicated process. It is important to select a method of relaxation that fits for you. Some relaxation strategies might be called "deep relaxation strategies," while others that can be learned much more quickly are often referred to as "brief relaxation methods." We now review some examples of each type of relaxation.

DEEP RELAXATION STRATEGY:
PROGRESSIVE MUSCLE RELAXATION (PMR)

Progressive muscle relaxation (PMR) is a deep relaxation procedure that involves the tensing and releasing of the major muscle groups throughout the body. To master the principles of PMR, I recommend that you put an audiotape into your tape player and record yourself reading the following deep relaxation dialogue, all the while using a gentle, evenly measured voice. You may even wish to play some soft, relaxing music in the background.

Once you have finished your relaxation tape, find a quiet place where you can go and completely relax your body. Structuring the environment so that it supports your relaxation is important. Close the window blinds, turn off the lights and pull the plug on the telephone. Find a comfortable chair where you can lean back and uncross your arms and legs. Once you are comfortable, begin playing the tape you have made, following the instructions closely. After doing this regularly for several weeks, it will become much easier to relax your muscles. Begin focusing on the muscles that get particularly tense when you are angry. For example, if your shoulders tense up when you are angry, you can spend extra time working on relaxing your shoulders.

The following is a relaxation dialogue taken from the suggestions of Kenneth Lichstein, Ph.D. author of the book Clinical Relaxation Strategies. The purpose of this exercise is to induce relaxation by tensing and then releasing muscles. Tense the muscles according to the instructions that are given, hold them for about seven seconds, and then release. What follows is the deep relaxation dialogue you will want to record:

RELAXATION DIALOGUE:

"Please keep your eyes closed throughout the following procedure. I am going to ask you to tense the different muscles of your body, and when I do, tense them as much as you can until I say 'relax.' Then let your muscles return to the resting state immediately. Throughout the tensing and relaxing phases, it is most important to focus all of your attention on the sensations coming from your muscles."

> --Tense the muscles of your right hand and forearm by clenching your right fist. Keep it tight, feel the strain, the tension, the muscles are working so hard, and relax (7 seconds). Relax completely, relax immediately. Just give up control of the muscles and let them lie there quietly.

--Tense the large muscle in your right upper arm, the biceps, by bending your right arm at the elbow and flexing. And relax (7 seconds).

--Tense the muscles of your left hand and forearm by clenching your left fist. And relax (7 seconds).

--Tense the muscles of you left biceps in the same manner that you did your right. And relax (7 seconds).

--Tense the muscles of your forehead by raising your eyebrows as high as they will go and wrinkling your forehead. And relax (7 seconds).

--Tense the muscles in the middle portion of your face by closing your eyes tightly and wrinkling your nose. And relax (7 seconds).

--Tense your lower face by pressing both your lips and teeth together, and pressing your tongue against the roof of your mouth. And relax (7 seconds).

--Tense your neck. There are many muscles that act to pull your neck in different directions. You can tense all of these at the same time by trying to move your neck in four directions simultaneously. Doing this, your neck will not be able to move in any direction, although you may feel a shaking or tremor there since all the muscles are tugging against each other. And relax (7 seconds).

--Before going on, and to help deepen the relaxation, I want you to take five deep breaths and hold each one for about five seconds. Softly say the word 'relax' as you exhale and quickly scan your body to seek out and deepen the feelings of relaxation.

--Tense the large muscles in your upper back by pulling your shoulders back as far back as though you were trying to touch them behind you. And relax (7 seconds).

--Tense the muscles of your chest and abdomen by simultaneously pulling your shoulders in front of you and tensing your stomach. And relax (7 seconds).

--Tense the muscles in your right upper leg. Similar to the neck, the thigh has many muscles that work in opposition. You can tense all of these at the same time by raising your right leg about an inch and making your right thigh hard. And relax (7 seconds).

--Tense your right calf by pointing your right foot and toes forward. Don't strain too hard as this muscle has a tendency to cramp. And relax (3 seconds).

--Tense your right ankle and shin by pointing your right foot and toes toward your face. And relax (7 seconds).

--Tense your left thigh by raising your left leg about an inch and making it rigid. And relax (7 seconds).

--Tense your left calf by pointing your left foot and toes forward. And relax (3 seconds).

--Tense your left ankle and shin by pointing your left foot and toes toward your face. And relax (7 seconds).

FINISH RELAXATION DIALOGUE

Once you have mastered the principles of relaxing your body, you are ready for the real work to begin. The next step is to learn to relax without the aid of the tape. After you are able to achieve a relaxed state without listening to the tape, you can reach the same levels of relaxation across different settings. You may begin repeating in your mind "Tense your neck; and relax", as you are in a heated discussion with your partner, or talking with your boss. As you become increasingly good at relaxation you will be able to use pieces of this procedure to help calm yourself down no matter what situation you might be in. You can begin as you go throughout the day to tense and relax the same muscles that you relax when you review the dialogue. When you are in situations in which you would normally anger yourself, you may begin to tense and release, particularly those muscles that tense when you anger yourself. This process allows the body to relax, even in the presence of activators.

So, to review the way the process works: 1) you create, using the dialogue in this book, your own relaxation tape; 2) practice using the tape to relax your entire body; 3) gradually move from using the tape to just repeating the different commands in your mind and achieving relaxation; 4) focus your attention on the muscles that reliably tense up when you anger yourself; and 5) become good at using this strategy in situations in which you ordinarily anger yourself.

DEEP RELAXATION STRATEGY:
MANAGING ANGER BY USING IMAGERY

Imagery is a technique that is closely tied to the use of relaxation. It has been used as a means of relaxing the body and mind for more than 2000 years. The use of imagery has traditionally involved picturing in the mind a pleasant scene that was once experienced. As the details of the scene are recalled, it is easy to induce some of the same comfortable feelings that were experienced when the scene was encountered for the first time.

It is often helpful, when attempting to re-experience a calming scene, to attempt to remember the odors, sounds, thoughts and feelings that were experienced during that scene the first time. For example, if I were seeking to use imagery in order to help manage my anger, I might remember a very peaceful experience I once had while observing the sun set on a beach in Australia. I would attempt to remember the scene in vivid detail, including the lapping of the surf against the shore, the muted cries of seagulls drifting overhead, and the fading yellow/orange color of the sun. By going through this process of recalling pleasant images, it is very unlikely that the anger you may have been experiencing will remain. The positive imagery replaces the old anger-producing beliefs with new feelings of calm and tranquility.

Jerry Deffenbacher, Ph.D., has suggested another use for imagery. Instead of picturing positive scenes, it is possible to use the images of anger-inducing situations in order to increase our tolerance for various activators, and learn to calm our bodies. This process involves several stages.

> --Learn some form of relaxation (like PMR) that allows you to calm your body when it is beginning to get aroused.
>
> -- Carefully think about situations in which you are likely to get angry. Those might include interactions with others, episodes when you are driving, or any one of a number of different scenarios.
>
> --Construct an anger image. Picture yourself in a situation where things happen that you often anger yourself about. Picture your own reaction. Imagine the changes occurring in your body; imagine your thoughts; imagine the actions that you take as you make yourself angrier and angrier.
>
> --As you imagine the anger scene, and you move into the 5-10 range of the Internal Anger Scale, begin calming yourself by using the relaxation techniques you have learned.

--Practice this process repeatedly. Begin to use the same calming tools in real-life situations that you use to calm yourself in the imaginal anger-inducing situations.

This is a process that helps you practice, in your own mind, dealing with unpleasant things that either have, or may occur, in real life. It is a form of deliberately exposing yourself to various activators in order to help you learn how to deal with those experiences effectively when you actually face them.

Whenever I am angering myself, especially when I am driving, I call up the image of the local newspaper with the headline reading, "Famous Anger Management Doctor Stuck In Traffic Jam Kills Two!" The prospect of having the whole world know that I got angry, and then behaved aggressively, stops my anger dead in its tracks. By using imagery to focus on the consequences of your anger, you can get better control of it.

CONTROLLED BREATHING

Many of the phrases used to describe anger, and efforts at reducing it, include the notion of temperature. "He's a hot head." or "He needs to chill out." are often heard. Interestingly, it appears as if our brains literally do become hotter the angrier we get. That's why, when practicing CB, it is important to inhale through your nose which has a cooling effect on the brain that breathing in through the mouth does not!

Of all the physiological techniques designed to address excessive anger, controlled breathing (CB) is clearly my favorite. It's my favorite for two reasons. First, it is easy and quick to learn. Second, it is highly portable. That is, you can use it any time and in any place. CB involves replacing the rapid breathing that typically accompanies anger with slower, deeper breaths. By forcing you to monitor your breathing closely, CB can also be helpful by taking your mind at least partially off a given activator. Taking deep breaths also increases the levels of carbon dioxide in the bloodstream, which produces a lethargic, calming feeling in the muscles and body. CB is both simple and effective. Here is how to do it:

1.) Move away from the activator you are angering yourself over. This is the old idea of getting out of the situation and "counting to ten," or giving yourself a Personal Time Out (PTO).

2.) Tell yourself forcefully: "Regulate your breathing!"

3.) Putting one hand on your stomach and one hand on your chest, slowly and smoothly breathe in through your nose counting to yourself (1 second-2 seconds-3 seconds). Keep the hand on your chest as still as possible, allowing only the one on your stomach to move. Pause for a second. Then exhale through your mouth counting to yourself (3 seconds-2 seconds-1 second). Exhale slowly and smoothly. Continue this process until you feel calmer. For most people, this will take a relatively short period of time, approximately 1 minute.

One thing I have consistently noticed when working with angry clients is how their general body tension diminishes during the course of a session. Often they come into the session "all puffed up" with their anger and then we begin exploring their anger-producing beliefs more closely. As the beliefs are exposed, and disputed, their muscles become less tense, their breathing more regular, and a sense of calm comes over them. Look for this same experience the next time you use PMR, CB or after successfully disputing your anger-producing beliefs!

SUGGESTED HOMEWORK:

A.)   Complete one "Managing Your Anger" form as found in the Appendix.

B.)   Practice the Controlled Breathing (CB) technique at least once a day.

C.)   What well-known chemical is released when you anger yourself?
        _____

D.)   When practicing CB, it is important to keep the hand on your _____
        still, while allowing the hand on _____ to move.

E.)   Name two physical warning signs that occur before you become angry.

        1.)_____
        2.)_____

F.)   Taking a PTO is designed to help you_____
        _____

G.)   It's important to _____ taking a PTO before you *really* need to take one.

H.)   After taking a PTO, you need to work on changing your anger-producing
        _____.

CHAPTER FIVE

ANGER AND AGGRESSION: CHOOSING THE ASSERTIVE OPTION

Before discussing assertiveness, let's clear up one point. There is no genetic basis for assertiveness. Client's have told me, as we discussed how they might handle a problem more assertively, "Well Brad, that's just not me. That's not something I can do." Nonsense! The ability to behave assertively is not something you have, or don't have, from the moment the doctor spanks your little behind and welcomes you into the world! Assertiveness is a *skill* that can be broken down into specific behaviors and *learned by anyone*. Just like the ABC's of REBT for your anger, assertiveness needs to be practiced daily.

From the diagram below it is clear that I am proposing a relationship between anger and aggression, as well as one between irritation and assertiveness. When you are angry, you are *more likely* to behave aggressively, either physically and/or verbally. By converting anger into irritation, you are *less likely* to behave aggressively and *more likely* to behave assertively. Why is this important? For many people reading this book it is not their anger that gets them into trouble, rather, it's that they *act* aggressively when angry. By converting anger into irritation, you reduce the likelihood of engaging in those behaviors that get you into trouble!

What are aggressive and assertive behaviors? They are two of the four general types of behaviors available to all human beings. The other types of behaviors being passive and passive-aggressive. Let's look at the characteristics each of type of behavior separately.

Angry people recognize the characteristics of *aggressive behaviors* immediately. Examples of aggressive behaviors include hitting things, hitting other people,

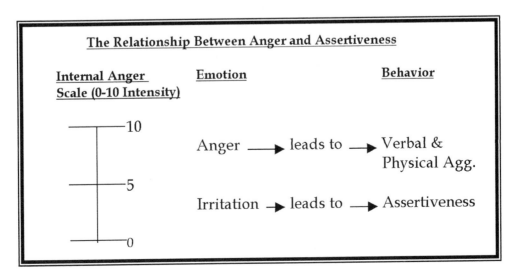

verbally "beating other people up" and threatening people. Just as anger-producing beliefs are demanding and commanding in nature so, too, are aggressive behaviors. They are designed to intimidate and control others regardless of the costs. When behaving aggressively you are likely to speak in a loud voice and "get up in the other person's face" while making your demands.

Passive behaviors are the opposite of aggressive behaviors. Instead of harming others either physically or verbally, you allow others to run you over without protesting. Instead of stating your thoughts, feelings and wishes, you remain silent and *allow* others to push you around. Passive people often apologize for things they didn't do, and say "Yes" when they really want to say "No!" When asked what they would like to do they frequently respond, "I don't know. Let's do whatever you want to do." These people often speak with very soft voices and have trouble maintaining eye contact. Angry, aggressive people view passive individuals as wimps or weaklings.

Passive-aggressive behaviors are a bit more complex because they involve an indirect expression of anger. Here is an example. You and your wife have an argument in the morning before you go to work. During the day you decide to just "drop it." You return home and begin talking to your wife who is in the kitchen. "Hi honey! How did your day go?" Without turning around she says harshly, "Fine!" "So what did you do today?" "Nothing!" she growls. By this time you sense that something is very wrong. "Geeze honey, is everything OK?" "Yes!" she exclaims, slamming the cabinet door and leaving the room. Now do you recognize passive-aggressive behavior? Rather than coming out and saying that she is still angry over the argument from that morning, she lets you know how she is feeling through her tone of voice and other behaviors. Sulking, pouting, giving someone "the silent treatment" or the "cold shoulder," are all examples of passive-aggressive behaviors.

> *Passive-aggressive behaviors have a corrosive effect on relationships by turning communications into an unpleasant game. Let me explain. In the above example, the wife has clearly made herself angry, yet she refuses to deal with it directly. Rather, she sets out to punish her husband by giving him "the cold shoulder." An analogy I like to use is that she has picked up her rod and reel and gone fishing but, in this case, the fish is her husband! With her first passive-aggressive response she casts the line out. With his first follow up question he takes the bait as she sets the hook and begins reeling him in! Ending this game involves no longer taking the bait, which means that in this case the husband would no longer reward her behavior by continuing to ask her, "What's wrong?" My advice to the husband would be that he approach his wife and say, "Honey, I can see that you are upset about something. When you're ready to talk about it, let me know and we'll get together to work this problem out." Game over.*

Assertiveness involves describing a specific problem situation to the activator. More often than not, the specific problem situation has something to do with the activator's behavior. You then tell the activator how you have *chosen* to feel about the problem situation (usually angry). Next, you tell the activator how their behavior affects you. Finally, you ask the activator to do something different that you would *prefer*. In essence, *assertiveness is where you request that the activator change him or her self*. Notice that when you behave aggressively you are trying to *compel* the activator to change or do what you think he or she *should*, *must* and *ought to* do. With assertiveness, the goal is to *influence* the activator to change him or her self by suggesting a new behavior that you would *prefer*.

Assertiveness involves the following four steps:

STEP 1.)   Describe the problem situation to the activator (usually the activator's behavior).

THEN

STEP 2.)   Tell the activator how you *choose* to feel about their behavior.

THEN

STEP 3.)   Tell the activator how their behavior affects you.

THEN

STEP 4.)   Suggest a new behavior to the activator that you would *prefer*.

Here is an example most women can associate with ... getting their male partners to replace the seat after using the toilet! A woman might try the aggressive approach ("If I fall in one more time, I'm going to kill you!"), the passive approach ("That's OK honey, I don't mind falling into the toilet at three in the morning."), or the passive-aggressive approach (A scream from the bathroom. "What's wrong honey?" "NOTHING!!!!!!").

This is how it would sound if the woman in the above scenario tried the assertive approach:

STEP 1.)   "Honey, when you don't put the seat down after using the toilet,

STEP 2.)   I *choose* to feel very angry,

STEP 3.)   because it's unpleasant falling into a cold and wet toilet at three in the morning.

STEP 4.)   In the future, I would prefer that you put the seat back down when you finish using the toilet."

Let's briefly look at Step 2, which puzzles many people until it is explained. In traditional assertiveness training, at Step 2 you are asked to tell the other person how their behavior *made* you feel. So, if you were using that model, the exchange would sound like this:

STEP 1.)   "Honey, when you don't put the seat down after using the toilet,

STEP 2.)   you *make me* very angry."

Do you see the problem? Traditional models of assertiveness place responsibility for the creation of your feelings on the other person. This is the old *A* $\xrightarrow[causes]{}$ *C Connection* we discussed earlier and represents your former, unhelpful way of thinking. By phrasing it the way I propose in the example, you again remind yourself that *you create your own emotions*, including anger. To the extent that your speech reminds you of the fact that you create your own anger, it reinforces that notion in your beliefs.

A second reason for phrasing it that way has to do with how the other person may react to your assertive message. While it is not the case that your assertive statement can *cause* them to react a certain way (e.g., angrily), you still need to be aware of the fact that some ways of saying things are more helpful than others. As my mother used to say, "It's not what you say, it's how you say it." By acknowledging that you made yourself angry over the activator's behavior, you are accepting responsibility for your emotions, rather than pointing fingers and trying to place blame on the activator. By not pointing fingers and placing blame, you decrease the chances that the activator will respond defensively, and increase the likelihood that he or she will hear your request asking them to change their behavior.

Assertiveness involves more than just these four steps. Were the wife in the above example to make her assertive statement, all the while using a very soft voice, shuffling her feet and looking at the floor, it would send a very mixed message. It would tell her husband that she really didn't take the request seriously and, if she doesn't take the request seriously, why should he? It's important to establish a firm and confident stance when delivering your assertive message. You should look the other person directly in the eyes and use a tone of voice that conveys confidence. You need to communicate that this matter is important to you, and that you want them to act on your request for change.

BEING ASSERTIVE WITH "TOUGH CUSTOMERS"

While many people will appreciate your assertiveness, others will respond with anger or tears designed to throw you off track. These are the people I refer to as "tough customers." The crucial point to remember here is that if someone becomes angry or tearful over your assertive statement, *they have chosen to either anger or upset themselves.* You are not so powerful that you can create their discomfort.

If you've stuck with the book this far, chances are good that you now accept the notion that you create your own emotional distress (usually anger) based on how you think about the activators in your life. If you create your own emotional distress based on how *you* think about things, isn't it only logical that *others create their own emotional distress based on how they think?* Of course it is!

Remember that *it is what the other person tells him or her self, about your assertive message that creates his or her anger and upset!* They can end their anger and upset anytime they choose simply by altering how they think about your assertive message.

SOME FINAL THOUGHTS ON ASSERTIVENESS

Many people believe that they have behaved assertively *only* if they get what they are requesting. The woman in the above example might think that she has behaved assertively *only* if her husband begins putting the toilet seat down. That's not true. Simply because we assertively ask for something does not mean we automatically get it. *The success in behaving assertively comes from the asking itself!* If you get what you ask for, that's great. Even if you don't get what you ask for, you can still congratulate yourself for behaving assertively.

One other point needs to be made about assertive behavior. Clients who move from anger and aggression, to irritation and assertiveness, consistently report feeling better about themselves when they abandon aggression and use assertiveness in its place. Think about those instances where you behaved aggressively in the past. Whether you got what you demanded or not, didn't you almost always feel guilty and ashamed of your aggressive behavior? When you behave assertively you not only increase the chances of getting what you want but, even if you don't, you still avoid feelings of guilt and shame over your behavior.

SUGGESTED HOMEWORK:

A.) Complete one "Managing Your Anger" form as found in the Appendix.

B.) Using the "Assertiveness Worksheet" found in the Appendix , a completed example of which is supplied, review the steps involved in behaving assertively and then complete one example where you practiced behaving more assertively during the past week. Here's a tip. Use the activator you write about in the "Managing Your Anger" form as the basis for STEP 1 of the "Assertiveness Worksheet." This way you can see how these two exercises work together as you convert anger into irritation, and then aggression into assertiveness.

C.) TRUE/FALSE: You can make other people angry with your assertive requests.

D.) The approach towards assertiveness discussed in this chapter differs from traditional approaches in that _____
_____
_____
_____.

E.) TRUE/FALSE: You have behaved assertively *only* if you get what you are asking for.

F.) Passive-aggressive behaviors involve an _____ expression of anger and include such behaviors as the "cold shoulder," the "_____ treatment, " and pouting.

CHAPTER SIX

ANGER AND PROBLEM SOLVING

Life is a series of problems. Do we want to moan about them or solve them?

The Road Less Traveled, M. Scott Peck, M.D.

Activators are frequently problems in our lives that need to be solved. One way to think about the relationship between anger and problem solving is by imagining the kind of blinders placed on a horse's head. The blinders are designed to prevent the horse from seeing anything but what lies straight ahead. Anger has the same limiting effect, but in this case on your problem solving skills.

Anger interferes with your ability to solve life's many problems by narrowing your field of view so that all you can see are solutions laying straight ahead. Unfortunately, those solutions tend to be the most simplistic available. They also tend to be the ones associated with some form of aggression or attempt at controlling others. By converting anger into irritation, you peel away the blinders and allow yourself to see the whole range of possible solutions to your problems--including non-violent and non-controlling solutions. From the diagram below it is clear that anger leads to poor problem solving, while irritation results in improved problem solving. By converting anger into irritation, you increase your chances of solving life's myriad problems.

The Relationship Between Anger and Problem Solving

Internal Anger Scale (0-10 Intensity)	**Emotion**		**Problem Solving**
10	Anger	leads to	▼ 'ed Problem Solving
5	Irritation	leads to	↑ 'ed Problem Solving
0			

A client once told me the story of how, in certain cultures, monkeys are used to help locate water supplies for the village. To attract the monkey a piece of fruit is placed in a cage. The monkey reaches through the cage's opening and grabs the piece of fruit. Grasping the fruit, the monkey is no longer able to pull free from the cage. The more furiously he tries removing his hand, the more trapped he becomes. All the monkey has to do in order to solve his problem is let go of the fruit, yet his anger blinds him to that solution. Isn't that the way anger blinds each of us?

THE FIVE STAGES OF EFFECTIVE PROBLEM SOLVING

Step One

Once you have converted anger into irritation, using the ABC's of REBT, you are positioned emotionally to begin solving problems. Effective problem solving involves five steps. Step One involves answering the simple question, "Do I have a problem?" There are three sources of information available to help you answer that question. Those sources are your:

> *Emotions:* If you are experiencing anger, chances are good that there are problems in your life needing to be solved.

> *Behaviors:* If you are yelling at or striking others, there are likely problems in your life needing to be solved.

> *Physical symptoms:* If you are experiencing constant muscle tension, headaches, clenched teeth, etc., chances are good that there are problems in your life needing to be solved.

You will recall seeing these three sources of information before, but in a different context. They are the three types of consequences you evaluate each time you complete a "Managing Your Anger" form.

The question of whether or not you have a problem can be answered either "Yes" or "No." If the answer is "No," the process stops. If the answer is "Yes," move on to Step Two, which requires you to accurately define the nature of the problem.

Step Two

Problem definition involves gathering as much information about the situation as you can. This allows you to understand the problem as clearly as possible. Separate facts about the problem from your opinions about it. It's also important to separate the person you are having the problem with from the problem itself. Feelings of anger or mistrust toward a person can keep you from clearly identifying the *real* problem. This is another reason why it is so important to convert your anger into irritation before trying to solve problems. Avoid making assumptions and jumping to conclusions either about the problem or about how others will respond to possible solutions. Always keep in mind what the most favorable solution of the problem would be *for you.*

Step Three

Once you've defined the problem, generate as many solutions to it as possible, *no matter how crazy some of those solutions might initially seem.* Another name for this process is brainstorming. Think of the first solution that comes to your mind and write it down. But don't stop there! As you generate more solutions, the possibility of identifying the best one increases. It's important *not* to consider the possible outcomes or consequences of implementing a solution at this point. The idea is simply to generate as many options as possible. Don't be afraid to ask others for possible solutions. Having a long list of solutions gives you something to return to if your first attempt at solving the problem fails.

My favorite story of how these first three steps are used together comes from a problem-solving group I conducted during my clinical training on an adult, inpatient psychiatric unit. In addition to the usual depressed and anxious patients, a psychotic patient joined the group one morning. When I asked if anyone had a problem they wanted to work on using the aforementioned steps the psychotic patient, in his mid-thirties, unshaven, and wearing a black motorcycle jacket, raised his hand and said, "Yeah, I've got a problem I want to work on." Having just told the group that these steps would work for any problem, I had to "put up or shut up" as it were. "OK," I said, "what's the problem you want to work on?" "My problem is with Dr. Nottingham," he replied. Dr. Nottingham being the psychologist who served as the unit's Program Director and who was responsible for my training.

Everyone in the group held their breath to see what would happen next. "Alright, let's define the problem," I suggested. "The problem I have with Dr. Nottingham is that he wears those ugly loafers with tassels," referring to my mentor's favorite choice in footwear. My straightforward response was, "Alright, now that we have defined the problem, how about generating some possible solutions. Who has some ideas?" At which point the patient looked at me, drew his right hand to his neck, and made an upward chopping motion. The patients gasped. Not wishing to appear unsettled, I calmly asked, "Well, I think I know what that gesture means to me, but why don't you tell me what it means to you?" "I could kill the bastard," he snarled.

Now, the question I have for you, as I did for members of the group at the time is, "Based on the definition of brainstorming you've just been given, did I include killing Dr. Nottingham as one possible solution to this patient's problem?" Absolutely! Brainstorming is an exercise in opening your mind to the *full range* of possible solutions to a problem. Clearly, killing Dr. Nottingham would have solved the patient's problem, although it would have set in motion a whole new set of even more serious problems! It's left to Step Four to begin the process of evaluating possible options.

Step Four

Once you have brainstormed as many options for solving the problem as possible, it's time to look at those options in the harsh light of reality. Here the task is to retain on your list only those options that help you achieve your goal without creating new, and perhaps even more serious problems. As you look down the list, it becomes obvious fairly quickly that many options will not survive "the cut." Those that do, however, become your working list of options. It is from that working list that you will begin choosing options to try out in Step Five.

Step Five and Beyond

Going through the above steps, and then failing to try out possible solutions in the real world, renders the entire problem solving process worthless. You need to find the courage to try the solutions you have devised. If you don't try out your solutions, the problem remains forever unsolved. To the extent that life's problems remain unsolved, you remain stuck in place as a human being.

> *A popular bumper sticker reads, "He who dies with the most toys wins." I've always been of the opinion that, "He or she who solves more of life's problems wins." Which do you think is right?*

One question that arises frequently is, "What do I do if, after trying all the reasonable solutions, I still don't solve the problem?" Two points need to be made here. First, when people talk about not being able to solve a problem, what they often mean is they don't *like* any of the range of possible solutions available for solving that problem. While I believe that all problems have solutions, not all solutions will be to our liking. Sometimes, when solving problems, we are forced to choose between the *lesser of two evils* and simply accept that outcome.

Second, when I ask the client which of the above steps he or she should return to, having failed to solve the problem, invariably he or she replies, "I need to go back to Step Three and generate some more options." While this might look like the right thing to do, it seldom yields any significant new options that actually solve the problem. What I recommend is returning to Step Two and redefining the problem. Once the problem is redefined, and a new set of options generated, the most suitable solution usually presents its self. An illustration of this process may be helpful.

Some years ago I purchased a car manufactured by a company that prided itself, at least in its advertising, on having the most satisfied customers in the automotive world. After leaving the dealership, I took my silver beauty home and, getting out a wax I had used for years, began removing from the rear bumper a few stray tar spots that had eluded the dealer's prep person. Upon awakening the next morning, and looking at the rear bumper, it became clear that, in each place where I had used the wax, some of the paint had been removed. Most unhappy, I drove to the dealer only to hear that they would be happy to have the bumper repainted but, other than that, there was nothing they could do. I went home and resolved to work on how I thought about this situation so as to deal with my *irritation*.

Two weeks later, while washing the car, my wife and I noticed further problems in the paint. Back in the car again for a return to the dealership. The answer remained the same, they would be happy to have it repainted but, other than that, their hands were tied. Practicing what I preach, I got back in my car and started disputing my now anger-producing beliefs.

The final straw came three days later. During the first rainstorm since purchasing the car, I turned on the windshield wipers only to have one of the blades scratch a perfect semi-circle in the windshield. Back to the dealership. This time I stated flatly to the sales manager, "I think I've purchased a lemon and would like you to replace the car." He looked at me, got the calculator out of his desk, and pronounced that he would be happy to replace the car, but only if I wrote him a check for $4000.00 to cover the amount the car had depreciated during the three weeks I owned it. When I protested that the figure was unacceptably high, he asked what I would be comfortable with. Since I had indeed used the car during that time, I suggested a figure between $500.00 and $1000.00. That offer was unacceptably low from his perspective and so we were stuck.

From the standpoint of using the five problem-solving steps we just covered, I had tried all the possible solutions I could think of and none got me the outcome I desired--a new car for between $500.00 and $1000.00. After leaving the dealership, I began asking myself whether or not I had defined the problem correctly. To that point I had defined it as being between the dealership and myself. It was not until I got home that I realized that the problem was not between the dealership and myself, but rather between the manufacturer and myself. Once redefined along those lines, I called the manufacturer's 800 number and spoke with a charming woman in customer relations who announced that she would investigate the complaint immediately. The next morning, before I could inform the sales manager of what I had done, he called and announced that a version of my car was being brought to the dealership later that day and that it would be mine in return for a check for $1000.00. Problem solved.

Not angering myself during this whole process played a crucial role in allowing me to correctly redefine the problem, and then generate new options. It also prevented me from destroying my relationship with the sales manager. Had I angered myself, I likely would have behaved in a verbally aggressive manner towards him, making it even less likely that he would respond favorably to my request. Managing your emotions, in this case anger, and using the five steps for effective problem solving, helps you move beyond complaining about life's problems, to actually solving them.

SUGGESTED HOMEWORK:

A.) Complete one "Managing Your Anger" form as found in the Appendix.

B.) Complete one "Assertiveness Worksheet" as found in the Appendix.

C.) Complete one "Problem Solving Worksheet" as found in the Appendix. An example of how to complete this form is supplied for your review.

D.) When you have tried all the possible solutions at Step Four, it is important to _____ to Step_____, and then begin generating _____options.

E.) Anger puts _____ on your ability to solve problems.

F.) _____ is the process of generating as many options for solving a problem as possible, no matter how crazy they may initially seem.

CHAPTER SEVEN

SELF-DISCIPLINE BEFORE OTHER-DISCIPLINE:
THE ART OF BEING A PARENT

In self-discipline one makes a "disciple" of oneself. One is one's own teacher, trainer, coach, and "disciplinarian." It is an odd sort of relationship, paradoxical in its own way, and many of us do not handle it very well. There is much unhappiness and personal distress in the world because of failures to control tempers, appetites, passions, and impulses. "Oh, if only I had stopped myself" is an all too familiar refrain.

The Book of Virtues, William J. Bennett

It is often instructive to examine the origins of terms we use daily and think we understand. Self-discipline is such a term. Do we really understand what it requires of us in terms of how we live our lives and how we interact with others? The roots of the word discipline are found in the word disciple. To be a disciple means to be "One who embraces and assists in spreading the teaching of another." Thus, to be a disciple means not only to be a kind of follower, but also to be a teacher. From this perspective, self-discipline is a form of self-teaching or self-instruction. For most of us, the first disciples or teachers in our lives are our parents.

The title of this chapter, "Self-Discipline Before Other-Discipline: The Art of Being A Parent," implies that being a good parent involves, before anything else, practicing self-discipline (self-teaching) before attempting other-discipline (other-teaching). That is, parents need to first *instruct themselves* in self-management before attempting to instruct their children in self-management. Honestly, though, how many parents do you know who demonstrate self-discipline? Precious few. As a parent, do *you* operate from a position of self-discipline? Most likely not. How many parents believe that they are capable of disciplining their children when they are themselves undisciplined? The vast majority.

When parents bring their children to me to "fix" (as if I was some kind of psychological auto mechanic!) because the children are out of control, it is often the case that the parents lack self-discipline and are themselves out of control. I recall a mother and her twelve-year-old son. She appeared at her wit's end with the young man who refused to do his homework, stayed out with his friends beyond their agreed upon curfew, and was at times physically combative with her. "Dr. Barris, I just don't know what to do. I can't control him anymore." When I inquired about the child's home life things became much clearer. The boy's parents had divorced when he was eight years old. The father, who still lived in the same small town, had little to do with his son except for a brief visit during the holidays. Soon after the divorce the father moved in with his new girlfriend and, not long afterwards, had a child with her. The mother, for her part, was mostly unemployed except for an occasional temporary job. She took every opportunity to remind her son of his father's lack of support and blamed him for the fact that she couldn't "find another man" because "no man wants to take care of another guy's kid." And so it goes.

Is it any wonder that this child is unruly? Is it any wonder that this child is out of control? I am told by many clients, and participants in my anger management programs, that one of the things they value most about this book is its *consistent focus on how we are the source of many of our own problems.* So it is with parenting children. When you are having difficulty with your children, the first place you need to look for answers is in the mirror. Rather than focusing your energy on trying to change or control them, look to see how you can *change yourself.* If you cannot manage yourself, how can you teach your children manage themselves?

> *I liken the mind of a child to the soil of the most fertile garden the world has ever known. As children watch how the adults around them handle life's problems, it is akin to the adults spreading seeds upon that soil. Because the soil is so rich, every seed germinates and takes root. Just as every seed does not result in the development of a plant that is helpful to the garden, neither does every emotion and behavior displayed by adults result in children developing healthy emotions and behaviors of their own. Much of what this book describes involves weeding your "psychological garden" by identifying anger-producing beliefs and then pulling them out at the root. By practicing self-discipline parents reduce the amount of "weeding" their children need to do later in life.*

Throughout this book you have been learning how to manage your anger and aggression toward others. To the extent that you manage your anger, you are practicing self-discipline. Children see this self-mastery, respect it, and seek to emulate you. Once you have disciplined yourself then, and only then, are you ready to discipline your children.

DISTINGUISHING DISCIPLINE FROM PUNISHMENT

As the diagram on the next page suggests, I am proposing that a relationship exists between anger and poor parenting skills (i.e., relying primarily on *punishment* as the means of getting children to alter their behavior). A similar relationship exists between irritation and improved parenting skills (i.e., relying primarily on *discipline* as the means of getting children to alter their behavior). Disciplining children is not the same as punishing them. Punishment is a behavior growing out of anger. It is designed solely to reduce the likelihood of certain behaviors, with which you as a parent do not agree, from occurring in the future. When you are angry, and thinking only of punishing your child, you deprive them of the opportunity to learn as much as they can from their experiences. Helping them learn from their experiences is the goal of discipline.

Why do parents choose punishment over discipline? For many of the same flawed reasons we identified in Chapter One why people choose to anger themselves generally. Some parents make the connection that it was their punishment of the child that *made* him or her stop a particular objectionable behavior. When parents make this connection, it reinforces their tendency to use punishment because punishment *seems* to have worked. What has really occurred, however, is something much different. The punishment did not make the child do anything, rather, the child *decided* at some point that he or she no longer wished to experience further punishment and ceased the behavior you found objectionable. We now focus on some of the other important problems associated with using punishment as a means of getting children to alter their behavior.

Punishment, and the anger that underpins it, is based on the myth that you can control others—including your children. As you have been learning throughout this book, you have *0% control over the activators* in your life. The only things you can control are your own thoughts, feelings and behaviors concerning activators. As a parent, children will be one of the most significant activators in your life. When I suggest to parents that they *cannot directly control their children* they at first become perplexed, then agitated and fearful. They are perplexed because no one has ever suggested such a thing to them before and because they always believed that their parents had been able to control them. They become agitated and fearful because, after listening to my explanation of why it is not possible for them to control their children, they realize that what I am saying is true and that I have deprived them of the only parenting tool they knew how to use.

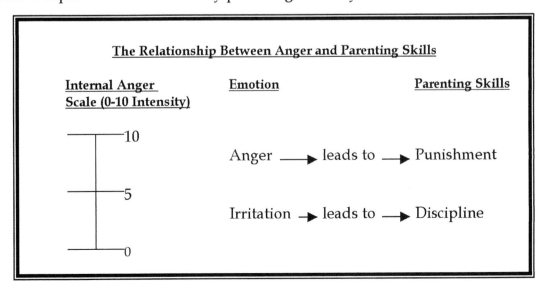

59

Since punishment is based on the myth that we can control others, it fails to recognize that others, including children, are *free* to make choices concerning whether or not to continue certain behaviors. You will recall my earlier observation that punishment works for *some* children, but only if that child decides that he or she no longer wishes to experience further punishment. Ultimately, the decision to either continue, or discontinue, certain behaviors resides exclusively with the child. In other words, *you cannot make a child do anything!*

Another problem with punishment, which I encounter frequently in my practice, involves what I have begun calling *punishment resistant* children. In these cases the parent's need to control their child is so great that each time the child resists those efforts, the parent *angers him or her self* and is forced to up the ante by increasing the punishment. Eventually these children, who have been punished all of their lives, no longer respond to any type of punishment—in essence, they have become punishment resistant. Having lost every possible privilege, and having experienced every form of physical punishment short of child abuse, they still refuse to alter their behavior.

At this point all parties to the problem are locked in a gigantic power struggle, or tug-of-war, with few options left. The child meets each tug of the rope by the parent with a corresponding tug. The only way out of this struggle is for the parent to find a way to "drop his or her end of the rope." Parents drop their end of the rope by challenging their anger-producing beliefs and by reminding themselves that they cannot control their children. These parents accept that children are free to make whatever choices they want, but they also *accept the responsibility of helping their children learn from the natural consequences growing out of their choices.*

The final problem with punishment stems from the fact that children often decide not to engage in certain behaviors, for which they have been punished in the past, *but only as long as the threat of punishment is immediately present.* Once the threat of immediate punishment is lifted, children often resume their objectionable behavior. This explains why "Junior" is such an "angel" at home, but a "holy terror" everywhere else.

If punishment is associated with all of these problems, what is a parent to do? As I've already suggested, parents need to first discipline themselves by effectively managing their anger, then they need to discipline (teach) their children by letting their children experience the *natural consequences* of their choices. Natural consequences are those consequences, not surprisingly, that *flow naturally* from the choices we make. For example, if your child does not set the alarm clock the night before an important morning test, the natural consequence of that choice would be missing the test and possibly flunking the class. Natural consequences are life's greatest teachers.

Every morning it was the same. The child would head for the door to catch the school bus with his mother running close behind, angering herself and demanding that he put his jacket on. "What can I do to get him to put his jacket on? We go through this every day!" she asked one day. I suggested that she let him experience the natural consequences of his decision not to wear a jacket and see how he handled the situation. The next day the child headed for the door to catch the bus without his jacket. Rather than chasing after him, his mother simply wished him a good day at school. As he got outside, it dawned on him that he was cold, at which point he went inside, found his jacket, and put it on. Ah, the power of natural consequences!

As a parent, your task is to guide your children by establishing a range of choices in any given situation, and then allowing them choose from within that range. The range of choices becomes greater the older the child gets, assuming that he or she has demonstrated good decision making in the past. When your children make wise choices, they get favorable results. When they make poor choices, they experience unfavorable outcomes. By interacting with them in this manner, you avoid the need to punish them and, instead, *teach* them self-discipline; i.e., how to make good choices and behave appropriately when no one is around to threaten punishment (e.g., parents, teachers, police, etc.).

Let's look at an example of how this would work. Johnny, age 15, has a math test coming up Friday morning. It's Wednesday afternoon and he has not begun studying for the test. Johnny also wants a new pair of sneakers from the mall this weekend. What do you do? Well, you could wait for Johnny to take the test and fail, at which point you could anger yourself over his poor performance, punish him by grounding him for two weeks, and hope he makes the connection between his poor performance and the punishment you have imposed. Or, you could propose this option:

"Johnny, I understand that you have a math test coming up Friday morning. Have you had a chance to start studying for it yet?"

"No, I've been too busy."

"Well that's okay, it's just that I remembered that you wanted me to take you to the mall this weekend to get a new pair of sneakers."

"Yeah, I still want to do that!"

"Let's make this deal. If you study for your exam, and get at least a B on it, I will assume that means you still want me to take you to the mall for

61

your sneakers. If you don't study for the exam, or don't get at least a B on it, then I assume you have *chosen* for me *not* to take you to the mall this weekend. I'll wait to see which *choice* you make."

A few points need to be made here. First, the way this situation is set up is perfectly consistent with the idea presented throughout this book that you cannot control other people, including your own children! One way you acknowledge this reality is by placing the choice squarely in the hands of the person who is really in control of making it, in this case Johnny.

Second, Johnny learns that all choices have consequences attached to them. As adults, I am convinced that the greatest gift we can give our children is the ability to function fully in the adult world when that time comes. You and I have to experience the consequences of our choices, so why shouldn't our children? The sooner they learn the connection between choices and consequences, the sooner they will become self-disciplined.

Finally, by having Johnny make the choice, you take yourself out of the position of being the mean, bad parent. In the past, if Johnny didn't study for the exam, or get at least a B on it, and you decided to punish him by not taking him to get his new sneakers, he would likely condemn you and announce, "I hate you! You won't let me have anything! It's because of you that I have to wear these ratty old sneakers to school!" With this new way of handling his discipline your response is ready made, "Johnny, I gave *you* the *choice* of whether or not to get the sneakers based on whether you studied for the exam and how well you did on it. When you did poorly, that meant *you chose* not to get the sneakers. If you need to be angry with someone, it seems that you need to be angry with yourself." End of discussion.

One last thought on the topic of punishment. As you have learned, punishment is designed to decrease certain behaviors. Rewards, conversely, are designed to increase certain behaviors. As a parent, it is important to realize that *rewarding desired behavior is always more powerful than punishing undesirable behavior*. Rather than looking for bad behaviors to punish, start spending more time looking for good behaviors to reward. My mother used to tell me, "You draw more flies with honey than you do with vinegar." Become one of those few parents who is good at giving out the honey, rather than being like the majority of parents whom are experts only at dispensing the vinegar. Your child will thank you!

SOME FINAL THOUGHTS ON PARENTING

As you have learned, your beliefs produce your anger. Not only can beliefs cause anger, but they can also create other unpleasant emotional experiences including *guilt*. One anger-producing belief that parents seem to hold on to more firmly than others takes the following form, "My children must love and obey me, and they must always be grateful for the sacrifices I make on their behalf." When children are not as loving as you think they *must* be, or when they don't obey you as they *should*, or when they are not as grateful for your sacrifices as you think they *ought to be*, then you make yourself very angry. The disputation for these anger-producing beliefs takes the form of asking yourself, "Where is it written that my children *must* love me, *must* obey my every command, and *must* be appreciative of everything I do for them?" The answer, obviously, is that none of these command's is written anywhere, except in your head! Would your relationships with your children be better if they were more loving, more obedient and more grateful? Absolutely! But must they treat you that way? Regretfully not.

Along the lines of the belief that children must treat their parents in the above ways is the belief that *parents must like and love their children equally*. Like other oft-repeated beliefs that are never examined, no one dares subject this belief to review lest they be labeled a "bad parent." The belief that parents *must* like and love their children equally is a fiction. Think about it for a moment, if the belief, "All parents must like and love their children equally" were true in the real world, that would mean that every parent loved and liked every child, and did so perfectly equally! When parents operate from this belief, it creates a breeding ground for feelings of guilt (a product of "shoulding-on" yourself rather than "shoulding-on" others) and denies the very real world fact that not all children are alike, nor are all children as easy to raise as others. Whether you accept this reality or not is immaterial. The fact remains, however, that we gravitate towards people who share our own likes and dislikes, whose temperaments are similar to our own, and whose way of seeing the world maps most closely onto our own. Put simply, we like people who are most like ourselves. To the extent that your child possesses a pleasant temperament, enjoys the things you enjoy, and views things in ways that are consistent with your own values, you will like and love him or her more. To the extent that your child possesses a difficult temperament, rejects the things you enjoy, and views things in ways that are antithetical to what you value, your liking and love for him or her will be lessened. Expecting that you would experience great liking and love for a child under the latter conditions is not realistic.

When I was in my late 20's my mother and I sat in her kitchen and had one of those rare conversations that "clears the air" for all time regarding a variety of topics. I recall angrily accusing her of preferring my brother to me when we were growing up because, as I had always heard, she should have treated us both the same! Her candid answer took me by surprise. "You're right Brad, I did favor your brother when you were growing up but you have to remember that, from the moment you were born, you were a pretty difficult person to be around. Where Roger was quiet, you were loud. Where Roger was easy going, you were demanding. If you are to be honest, you were a pain-in-the-butt growing up and your brother wasn't. Now do you understand why I liked Roger better than you?

In the next chapter we discuss in detail the "fallacy of unconditional love." Let me anticipate that discussion by saying that granting children unconditional love is just as problematic, if not more so, than granting it to an adult. Unconditional love given to children teaches them that there is nothing they can do, within the context of the parent-child relationship, that can severely damage or even destroy that relationship. *Love always needs to be conditional, even for children!*

SUGGESTED HOMEWORK:

A.) Complete one "Managing Your Anger" form as found in the Appendix.

B.) Complete one "Assertiveness Worksheet" as found in the Appendix.

C.) This chapter emphasizes that, in order for parents to discipline their children, they must first _____ themselves.

D.) True/False: Discipline is designed to "teach" children.

E.) The next time you anger yourself over something your child either did, or didn't do, complete one "Take A Poll" worksheet as found in the Appendix. An example of how to complete this form is supplied for your review.

F.) Discipline grows out of _____, whereas punishment grows out of _____.

G.) Rewarding_____behavior is always more powerful than _____bad behavior.

CHAPTER EIGHT

THE AFTERMATH OF ANGER: REBUILDING RELATIONSHIPS

No emotion disrupts and destroys relationships as completely as anger. When a loved one has problems with clinical depression or severe anxiety, it's easy to empathize with that person and stand beside him or her as they work to resolve their emotional distress. It is not that way, however, with anger. When exposed to chronically angry people we do everything in our power to avoid them. Empathizing with an angry person is not easy because their anger is so toxic that all we can do is plan our escape from them.

> *One client, while discussing how his anger had destroyed relationships with his wife and children, observed that it had also destroyed his relationship with himself. "You know Brad, I hate the person I've become because of my anger. I don't even really know who I am anymore, except that I am one very angry person."*

Now that you've acquired the skills to better manage your anger, it's time to try and rebuild the relationships damaged over the years. Before showing you how to rebuild those relationships, a cautionary note needs to be sounded. As you will learn later in this chapter, *not all relationships can, **or should**, be rebuilt*. Just because you have changed by becoming less angry does not mean that others *must* open their lives to you again. For some relationships the depth and breadth of the damage caused by your anger is too great to overcome. In those cases all you can do is accept the sadness accompanying the realization that the relationship is forever lost. For other relationships, the best you can do is make a sincere effort to demonstrate how you have changed, and *hope* that the other person is willing to try again. Despite your desire to control the outcome, the ultimate decision whether or not to resume the relationship always resides with the person who has received your anger. As a friend once told me, "Only the injured can forgive."

An unfortunate aspect of modern life is what I call the "tendency toward complexity." This is the notion that unless something is complex it cannot have value or be true. Where once we prized simplicity and elegance in our explanations for why things are a certain way, now all explanations must take on a labyrinthine quality to be considered valid. Unfortunately, no where is this tendency toward needless complexity more evident than in how psychology tries to help people understand basic human relationships.

Successful relationships are *not* the result of *secret factors* that you can only learn from expertly trained therapists. Rather, successful relationships are the result of keeping in mind certain basic principles, the most important of which I refer to as the "Scorecard Principle."

THE SCORECARD PRINCIPLE:
HEALTHY vs. PATHOLOGICAL LOVE

At some point in the history of Western civilization, people began believing in a notion called *unconditional love*. I gather from this term that they mean a form of love not conditional on other factors, including the behaviors of the person they are in love with. This is love "with no strings attached." How many times have I heard women who are being abused by their husbands, when asked why they remain in the marriage, respond "Because I love him." When asked for their *definition of love,* they look at me as if I am crazy, or as if I had just dropped in from another planet! "A definition of love? Why love is just, ah, love! It's what I *feel* toward my husband regardless of what he does to me. I love him unconditionally." To believe in unconditional love is to establish the conditions necessary for a *pathological, or sick, type of love*. Affording anyone, much less someone who is abusing you, unconditional love is akin to giving him or her *carte blanche* to continue that abuse. The only way out of such a pathological love relationship is to live according to the "Scorecard Principle" which is based very much on a belief in the necessity of *conditional love*.

Don't be naive or deceive yourself. Healthy relationships are built on the simple notion that *we love people who do things for us that we value*. From this perspective, our love for others is, in all respects, conditional. What this statement lacks in romance and fantasy, it more than makes up for in truth and reality. In healthy relationships, the parties have clearly drawn mental "scorecards" where they keep track of the positive things their partner does for them, along with the negative things. As the positive side of the scorecard grows, so does their love for their partner. As the negative side of the scorecard mounts, so does their love for their partner diminish.

When I tell this to clients who believe in unconditional love they scoff and declare my view of love and relationships to be unromantic, selfish or (God forbid!) self-centered. They act as if there were something inherently wrong with looking out for one's own well being within the context of a loving relationship! Since schooling as a psychologist involves training in the scientific method, I usually invite the skeptical client to test out my theory by undertaking the following simple experiment. After our session ends, they are to go home and tell their partner to *stop doing* those things for them that they value. No more breakfast in bed. No more foot rubs at the end of a long day. Nothing!

This embargo on doing valued things is to continue into the indefinite future. If their belief in unconditional love is true, they should report no decline in their feelings of love for their partner upon returning to my office at some future date. Based on my belief in conditional love, however, I would predict a rather noticeable reduction in their feelings of love towards their partner—and fairly quickly! Though I firmly believe that my guess would be proven correct, if the truth were told, none of my client's has ever accepted my offer to perform this experiment. The reason why? I suspect it is because they also know that what I am saying is true! When you stop doing for your partner the things he or she values, his or her love for you will depart on the same gossamer wings that once delivered it!

BUILDING RELATIONSHIPS VIA DEPOSITS AND WITHDRAWALS

Stephen R. Covey's excellent book, The Seven Habits Of Highly Effective People, discusses many of the simple truths we seem to have forgotten as a culture. To that book we now turn for guidance on building better relationships. Covey and I agree on the notion that loving relationships involve exchanging things of value between partners, as well as some means for keeping track of those exchanges. Where I use the metaphor of a scorecard, he introduces the notion that building relationships involves establishing an "Emotional Bank Account" with others.

The idea is simple and makes perfect sense. When we establish an account at the bank, we first make a deposit into the account. We continue making deposits into the account, which then collect interest and grow in value. Because we have made deposits in the past, and because the bank has proven itself worthy of our trust by always having our money available when we need it, we can withdraw funds in the future. Our relationship with the bank, therefore, is based on a series of deposits and withdrawals.

Interpersonal relationships develop in much the same way, albeit through a series of psychological or emotional deposits and withdrawals. Others view your angry outbursts towards them as withdrawals. Eventually, after making more withdrawals, without any corresponding new deposits to cover those withdrawals, your partner will likely close your emotional bank account and ask you to take your business elsewhere. This is what people mean when they refer to a relationship as "bankrupt." When your angry withdrawals for too long exceed your deposits, it will almost always be in the best interests of your partner to terminate the relationship.

If building relationships is based on a series of deposits and withdrawals, and anger is the primary means by which you make withdrawals, then the most important question you need to answer is, "How do I stop making angry withdrawals in my relationships and start making deposits into the Emotional Bank Accounts I have established with others?" Another way of looking at this question is, "How do I make my partner's love for me grow by feeling less angry and by doing the things he or she values?"

Obviously, using the techniques you have learned for better managing your anger is the necessary first step in rebuilding your relationships. By managing your anger you shift your attention from the debit (withdrawal) side of the scorecard to the deposit side. Rather than constantly worrying about not making further withdrawals, you can focus on how to make new deposits.

For Covey, the necessary first step in making deposits involves *understanding what the other person values.* Without truly understanding the other person, how can you know what he or she values and therefore what he or she considers to be a deposit? Too often the tendency is to assume that what we perceive of as a deposit is what the other person would also consider a deposit. Let's say you love golf, and receiving a dozen golf balls from your wife for your birthday constitutes a deposit on her part. Now, suppose your wife hates golf and you give her a dozen golf balls for her birthday. Have you made a deposit? Absolutely not! As a matter of fact, you've almost certainly made a withdrawal. The only reliable way to find out what another person values is by asking them!

If you have ever been involved in a relationship you learn rather early on that, as Covey says, *the little things become the big things.* Putting the toilet seat down, putting the cap back on the toothpaste, cleaning the hair out of the sink, are all little in the grand scheme of things. But if your partner deems them to be important, every time you fail to do one of those little things, you make a big withdrawal. Conversely, each time you perform these little acts of kindness, you make a sizeable deposit.

> *My wife is rather slow to awaken in the morning. Part of her ritual is to draw her bath and, while the tub is filling, pour herself a glass of soda. Early on in our marriage she asked if I would bring her soda to the bathroom since she was running late. Since that day, almost without fail, she is greeted each morning with a glass of amber liquid on the ledge surrounding the bath. A big thing? Certainly not. But enough to constitute a significant deposit on my part.*

Another way to make deposits involves *keeping the promises you make to others.* Put simply, keeping a commitment or promise is a major deposit; breaking a promise or commitment is a major withdrawal. If you don't believe this, simply look into the face of a child you have promised to take to the zoo when you tell him or her that they're not going. Can you think of a more significant withdrawal then making a promise to someone, about something that is important to them, and then not keeping that promise? My recommendation is that you get in the habit of not making promises unless you are very confident of your ability to keep them.

Whenever you enter into a new relationship, it is common for there to be a "honeymoon" period. During this time everything your partner does is considered a deposit and it's almost inconceivable that there would ever be any conflicts, or withdrawals, in your relationship. The reality is, however, that there will be withdrawals and they will oftentimes center on the *expectations* each party brings to the relationship. *By clarifying our expectations of others we make deposits in our relationships with them.* By allowing expectations to remain hazy or unclear we are establishing the conditions necessary for future withdrawals. The following story will illustrate my point.

A colleague of mine and I once discussed how he and his wife had decided to marry. He recounted how they had dated for a period of time and how he felt increasingly close to her. It appeared that, if the relationship continued on course, they would contemplate marriage. At one point in our conversation he stated, "And then I told her, 'Listen, this may sound terrible but I don't like children and, if we get married, you need to know that I do not want to have any children. If kids are important to you, then this relationship is not going to work.' " I was shocked by his candor and recalled thinking to myself, "What a jerk! How could he say that to her?" Over time, however, my reaction changed dramatically. You see, my friend was very aware of his dislike of children and he was equally sure that his position would not change with marriage. His *expectation* was that there would be no children born of this relationship. Imagine what would have happened if my friend had married this woman without ever discussing his views on children? It would have been a disaster, and possibly even a withdrawal large enough to end their marriage. Clarifying expectations takes considerable courage because, as in this case, it might have meant losing a relationship my friend valued greatly. Difficult to do? Yes. But well worth it in the long run.

It is inevitable that we will all make mistakes (withdrawals) in our relationships. When those occur, *a timely and sincere apology can transform a withdrawal into a deposit.* Few things make a more important deposit than an apology from the heart. Psychologically weak people are incapable of apologizing because, in their eyes, that would mean they had made a mistake. Acknowledging our mistakes takes considerable strength and courage. In addition to being timely and sincere, apologies must also include a commitment to the other person, and yourself, to no longer make the same withdrawal (mistake) in the future. I often tell my clients, "Listen to what people say, but trust what they do." Words of apology, without corresponding behavioral changes, are meaningless.

Hopefully by this time you are agreeing with my earlier observation that improving your relationships can be accomplished by following a few simple principles. Believing in conditional love is the first step, followed by finding out what your partner values, and then giving it to him or her on a regular basis. You will be amazed at how quickly their love for you grows!

BETTER COMMUNICATIONS USING REBT

When couples attend our anger management seminars they almost always remark how their communications improve after learning the new language associated with REBT. Why is that?

First, when each party to the relationship learns how to better manage his or her anger, it's only natural that their communications will improve. If you or your partner is angry all the time, lines of communication are effectively severed. When you both learn REBT, and acquire the skills necessary to reduce your anger, real communications can begin again.

Second, since you have been learning that you create your own anger, there is no finger pointing, blaming, or scapegoating others for your feelings. As each party to the relationship takes responsibility for his or her own thoughts, feelings and behaviors, they communicate forcefully to their partner that they are fully in control of themselves. They also position themselves to solve whatever problems they are confronting.

Third, because couples who learn REBT accept that they are not so powerful that they can create feelings in one another, they are more likely to discuss important aspects of their relationship. If I believe that something I want to discuss with my wife would "hurt her feelings" then, chances are, I will remain silent. If, however, I accept the fact that I cannot create feelings in my wife, that only she can make the decision whether or not to upset herself over what I might say, then I am more likely to discuss potential problems with her. Accepting responsibility for your own feelings, all the while allowing your partner to assume responsibility for his or hers, changes communications patterns in dramatic ways!

> *Chris and his wife Jackie were new to the anger management group. At one point Chris asked, "What do you do if you are the one that brings your partner down?" Bryan, an older group member, observed, "Chris, you need to get away from believing that you are the one who brings Jackie down. Only she can do that and you have no control over what she does. Rather than worrying about her, you need to take care of yourself. If you just took care of yourself that would be a twenty-four hour a day job. Believe me, you won't have any time left over to try and run Jackie's life."*

ANGER AND EMPATHY

Throughout this chapter we have outlined ways to improve relationships damaged by your anger. Another approach to improving relationships involves developing an ability to empathize with those who are on the receiving end of your rage.

In The Seven Habits of Highly Effective People, Stephen Covey gives this wise advice, "Seek first to understand, then to be understood." That is, strive first to understand the other person's position before trying to persuade them of yours. This represents Covey's call to each of us to develop our ability to empathize with others. Some specialists in the treatment of anger, including Jerry Deffenbacher, Ph.D., suggest that while angry people are aware of their own anger--including the behavioral and physiological changes accompanying their anger--they are much less aware of how their anger affects others. That is, they appear to have little understanding of, or empathy for, how others experience their anger (e.g., as an attempt to control their behavior, as an attempt to intimidate, as an attempt to frighten, etc.).

One way of developing empathy (i.e., putting yourself in the "other persons shoes") is by using the "Empathic Interview" I have developed based on a suggestion supplied by Dr. Deffenbacher. The interview, a copy of which is found in the Appendix, is designed to help you understand how other people think and feel when confronted with your anger, and why they choose to respond as they do. In this exercise, you interview a person you recently expressed anger towards. As you ask them questions, try empathizing or understanding exactly how they experienced being on the receiving end of your anger. The better you become at this exercise, the less likely you will be to express anger towards them in the future.

PREDICTING ANGER IN INTIMATE RELATIONSHIPS

Earlier in this chapter you learned about the importance of *clarifying expectations* within the context of your relationships. By clarifying expectations you make deposits into your partner's Emotional Bank Account and, even more importantly, lessen the probability of making very large withdrawals. People bring a variety of expectations into their relationships that may serve as potential flash points. How can you avoid the anger growing out of conflicting expectations? Not surprisingly, by avoiding conflicting expectations from the beginning!

By involving ourselves intimately in relationships we come to understand our strengths and weaknesses as human beings. Because these relationships are central to the human experience, and because the level of personal vulnerability is so great, intimate relationships are ripe with opportunities for personal growth, as well as fraught with opportunities for personal despair. For most failed intimate relationships, anger has played a central role in creating that despair.

Though I am often asked to counsel couples having difficulty managing anger within the context of their marriage, I no longer facilitate this type of therapy. I learned rather early on that, by the time a profoundly angry couple decides to seek help, it is usually too late to salvage their relationship. Someone once told me that it takes the average client two years before he or she decides to seek treatment for his or her psychological problems. If the same holds true for couples, that means they have usually spent those two years locked in angry accusations and non-stop arguments before ever entering a therapist's office. While I admire colleagues courageous enough to wade into this messy situation, I do not share their generally hopeful view concerning marital therapy in general, and am even less sanguine about marital therapy with profoundly angry couples.

Why do I hold out little hope for the ultimate repair of intimate relationships where anger has played such a large and destructive role? Why do these intimate relationships fail? Why do they invariably degenerate into a cycle of anger, bitterness and resentment? *I have little hope because, in my judgment, these relationships were destined to fail from the outset! And why were they destined to fail? Because the persons entering into these relationships never shared the same core beliefs and values.* These intimate relationships fail because, once the parties to the relationship recognize that they do not share the same core beliefs and values, one or both of them tries furiously to *control* their partner. The goal of that attempted control is to get the partner to change his or her core values and beliefs. When their partner does not yield to their efforts at controlling and changing them, the other party angers him or her self mightily and so the downward spiral begins. Each tries to control and change the other to no avail. Anger begets bitterness, which, in turn, begets resentment.

What do I mean when I speak of core values and beliefs? I mean those values and beliefs that are at the very center, or *core*, of an individuals psychological makeup. These are values and beliefs that the individual has about him or her self, and the world, that undergird and influence all their other beliefs and values. These are the values and beliefs that make Brad Barris uniquely Brad Barris and the reader uniquely him or her self. Hence the phrase core values and beliefs.

Because these core beliefs and values are central to our sense-of-self they are *very, very resistant to change*. Upon reflection, this resistance to change is perfectly understandable. Though many pay lip service to welcoming change in their lives, the reality is that humans are much more inclined to resist, rather than embrace, personal change. Change requires time, effort and energy. For most it means moving out of a comfort zone they know very well into a discomfort zone where everything is new and nothing is sure anymore. If we resist even minor changes, then imagine our reaction when our partner *demands* that we change those values and beliefs at the very core of our being!

Involving which areas of our lives do we develop core values and beliefs? In his no-nonsense book on relationships entitled The Three Faces Of Love, Paul Hauck, Ph.D., suggests a number of potential conflict areas couples involved in intimate relationships frequently encounter. While Hauck does not label them core values or beliefs, the problem areas he identifies encompass many areas where we tend to develop core values and beliefs. Those areas include, but are not limited to, financial responsibilities, the role of children, the role of church and religion, the role of family, devotion to work, the need for socializing and, lastly, the role of sex in the relationship.

> *The anger found in so many intimate relationships is ultimately the result of two factors. The first is the couple's failure to share similar core beliefs and values in the areas listed above. The second factor is related to the need of one or both of the partner's to change the other partner's core beliefs and values.*

When couples begin the dating process, their initial attraction to each other is "hard-wired" and primarily physical in nature. Why this is the case is perfectly understandable from an ethological perspective. Ethology is a broad field of study that includes, among other things, the study of animal behavior and how certain complex behaviors, including mating, are part of our genetic makeup. Ethology also looks at how those complex behaviors work in such a way as to guarantee the survival of a species. During the earliest days of our species, when the average life expectancy was brief to say the least, it was important that humans not spend a lot of time deciding whether or not they liked or loved a particular potential mate. At that point in our development, perpetuating the species was paramount and that meant that "couples" were unconcerned about their long-term relationship prospects and more concerned about their immediate need to procreate. Given those circumstances, getting to know and understand the core values and beliefs of your partner was not even a consideration!

As the human life span increased, the need to have children immediately so as to continue the species became less important. Where people had once been in relation to each other for short periods of time, now they remained together for extended periods of time. This lengthening of the period of relation required that people find a basis for the relationship beyond the immediate need to have sex and reproduce. The basis for continuing the relationship across time required that the couple share certain core values and beliefs like the ones mentioned above.

What happens when the parties to a relationship do not share core beliefs and values? The result is a nightmare-like existence characterized by ongoing interpersonal strife, conflict and anger. As noted earlier, these values are central to our sense-of-self. When your partner does not share, for example, your core value that children are an important part of marriage, you instinctively try to change his or her view. First subtly, then via a series of demands and commands, you try with all your might and energy to get your partner to share your core beliefs and values. Not surprisingly, the more you demand that they change their core beliefs and values, the more they dig in their heals and defend the *status quo*. The problem is not that you and your partner have certain core beliefs and values. Rather, the problem arises when those core beliefs and values differ and then when you demand that your partner's core beliefs and values change so they conform with your own.

> *Alice entered my office and began telling me about her marriage to Bob. She recounted how the first year had been total bliss. She could not have been happier and it seemed that they never disagreed about anything. Then, during the second year of their marriage, "Bob began to change." Where once there had been harmony, there was now discord. As a psychologist, I must believe that people are capable of changing. But I also know that certain elements of a person's basic outlook on the world are highly resistant to change. The chances of Bob changing as drastically as his wife implied were rather remote. That Alice had not done a very good job of "interviewing" Bob about his core values and beliefs during their brief courtship was much more likely. What seemed like a change in her husband was most likely his "true self" all the while. If only she had taken the time to get to know his true self!*

If you don't believe that the vast majority of the conflict and anger found in intimate relationships is due to these conflicting core beliefs and values simply ask yourself, "Would our relationship be better if my wife and I were 'on the same page' regarding the spending of money, the disciplining of the children, and whether or not our family will attend church this Sunday?" The answer, obviously, is "Yes."

For those individuals reading this book who are contemplating entering into an intimate relationship, it is imperative that you take the time (and that can mean years!) to get to know your potential partners core beliefs and values. If you share the same core beliefs and values, you can be relatively certain that there will be little anger and conflict in your life together. If your prospective partner does not share your core beliefs and values, then it is better to "bite the bullet" and move on until you find someone who does. Trust me, if you follow only this advice, you will thank me one day!

When assessing whether or not relationships will be relatively free of anger, I am reminded of the old Fram oil filter commercials on TV. The commercial opened with a mechanic holding a Fram oil filter in his hand and saying, "You can pay me $10.00 now to change your oil and filter or" and the camera would pan over to an engine being rebuilt, "you can pay me $1000.00 later to rebuild your engine." That notion of paying a little bit up front, in order to avoid a much larger charge down the road, is very good advice for people entertaining an intimate relationship. By getting to know your potential partners core values and beliefs up front, and deciding whether or not they are consistent with your own core beliefs and values, you save yourself much anger, pain and heartache down the road. You can pay a little now or a great deal later. It's your choice!

SUGGESTED HOMEWORK:

A.) Complete one "Managing Your Anger" form as found in the Appendix.

B.) Complete one "Assertiveness Worksheet" as found in the Appendix.

C.) According to the "Scorecard Principle" all love is _____.

D.) It is relatively easy to predict anger and conflict in a relationship. When the parties to the relationship do not share the same _____ _____, anger is likely to result.

E.) Name three of the five things Covey recommends doing in order to make deposits in your relationships.

    1.)_____
    2.)_____
    3.)_____

F.) Empathy is the ability to _____.

CHAPTER NINE

WHY ARE OUR CHILDREN SO ANGRY?

Example is not the main thing influencing others. It is the only thing.

Albert Schweitzer

Interacting with children and adolescents can be a profoundly humbling experience. What makes it humbling is that it confronts adults with the realization of how little we know about why these evolutionarily similar creatures behave as they do! The number one question I encounter when conducting anger management seminars for professionals is, "How do I treat angry children and adolescents?" The number one question I encounter when working with parents is, "How do we deal with our angry child or adolescent?" Most parents, educators and therapists agree that children and adolescents appear angrier today, and are more likely to act out their anger in aggressive ways. Whether this is true or not is open to debate. Why it may be true is the subject of much speculation and, if we are to be honest as a profession, *no one* knows with certainty why children and adolescents seem angrier today. It is in the spirit of the aforementioned humility that I add my own best guesses to the debate over why children and adolescents seem angrier today and what we can do to help them.

As you learned in the chapter on parenting, children observe and imitate the emotional and behavioral responses of the adults surrounding them. So it is with the emotional expression of anger and the behavioral response of aggression. While parents play an important role in this process, they are by no means the only sources of information for children regarding how to deal with anger. Though sports figures no longer consider themselves to be "role models," what do you think children and adolescents learn when they see the basketball player Dennis Rodman angrily kicking a cameraman along the sideline during a game? What example is being set for them when they see Indiana University basketball coach Bobby Knight yelling at an official or throwing a chair on to the court? They learn that adults get angry, behave aggressively and, especially in the case of Coach Knight, largely escape any negative consequences for their outrageous behaviors. Since both of these anger-mismanagement poster children are affiliated with generally successful sports programs, children also learn that as long as you win, angry and aggressive outbursts will likely be excused.

Children not only imitate the behaviors of adults, but also pay very close attention to the emotional and behavioral expressions of their *peers*. To the extent that their peers display anger and aggression, it is more likely that your child or adolescent will display similar feelings and behaviors.

Another factor contributing to an increase in anger amongst children and adolescents is related to the fact that today's adults seem angrier as well. Given that adults (except those reading this book!) have no understanding of where their anger comes from, they are in no position to educate their children concerning this emotion. To the extent that they do have an understanding, *adults teach children that other people make them angry*. While perpetuating that myth is good for my business, it merely creates the conditions for the next generation of angry children, adolescents and adults! Were adults to understand that they anger themselves, and then teach that to their children, the intergenerational transmission of anger might lessen, if not end.

> *When trying to illustrate the above point during my seminars I will ask someone in the audience, usually a woman, what her parents taught her about anger. After looking puzzled for a moment, I will help her out by asking, "Let's imagine you have an older sister named Sara. When you were children, you and Sara were playing with dolls in the back yard. One day Sara ripped the arms off your Barbie doll. You got very angry and ran inside. "What's wrong?" asked your mother. At which point you responded, "Sara makes me so mad when she tears up my dolls!" At this point I ask the person in the audience, "Would it be fair to assume that your mother, in an effort to calm you, asked the following question, "Well, wait a minute sweetheart, isn't it really what you think about Sara tearing up your doll that makes you so angry?" At which point the audience bursts into laughter upon realizing that no parent ever said such a thing to his or her child!*

Like adults, children and adolescents also learn early on that their anger appears to help them get what they *demand* from others. A mother came into my office one day complaining of her six-year-old son pitching a fit in the middle of Wal-Mart. Apparently the child had seen a particular cereal advertised on TV that morning and was determined to have his mother purchase it for him. The mother tried reasoning with him, including reminding her son that they were on a tight budget and didn't have enough money to purchase that particular cereal. The more she reasoned with him, the louder his wailing became. Needless to say other customers were watching this exchange and, according to the mother, she was absolutely convinced that they were damning her for being a "bad parent" because she could not *control* her son. Rather than endure the embarrassment of listening to his piercing screams, coupled with the "judgments" of the passersby, she gave in and purchased the cereal.

Were you the child in the above situation, what would you have learned? You don't have to be a psychologist to figure out that the son learned that getting angry enough, and screaming loudly enough, results in mom giving in to his demands. Is it any wonder then that, the next time he sees a new cereal on TV, this process begins anew? Now, his mother could attempt to solve this problem by preventing him from watching TV so that he doesn't learn about any new cereals; or she could hire a baby sitter each time she needs to go to the store and leave him at home. While these solutions might lessen her discomfort, would they really help her son learn self-discipline? The answer, obviously, is "No." What could she have done differently? I offered her two possible solutions. The next time her son had a temper tantrum in the store she was to kneel beside him and say, "Michael, if you want to continue screaming, there is really nothing I can do to stop you. But I do have some more shopping to get done. If you would like to stay in this aisle and scream some more, that's fine with me. I'll be back for you in a few minutes." This approach has two benefits associated with it. First, the mother is reminding herself that she has no direct control over her son's behavior. This lessens the chance that she will anger herself and either say or do something she later regrets. Second, it conveys to the child that she will not be held hostage by his poor behavior and will continue on with her tasks. Had the mother chosen this approach, I suspect her son would have quieted himself down rather quickly.

The other approach, which she did adopt, involves what psychologists call a paradoxical intervention. She kneeled next to her son and said, "Michael, what a wonderful screamer you are! But I'm sure you can scream louder and carry on even more than that. How about screaming louder for me. Would you do that for me? How about making even more of a fuss? I'll just sit here and we'll see if you can't scream and carry on even more." By asking her son to do *more* of what it was that she wanted him to *stop* doing, her son became confused and soon gave up his screaming. After all, it's no fun screaming if mom isn't going to reward the behavior by upsetting herself!

Key to the success of both of these strategies, however, was the mother's ability to manage her potentially angry response to her son's behavior. By not "shoulding-on" her son, she retained her composure and solved the problem. Remember the saying we introduced in the section on parenting—self-discipline before other-discipline! In this case, the mother was practicing self-discipline, which allowed her, in turn, to devise a response that helped teach her son self-discipline.

From a developmental perspective, dealing with children and adolescents is further complicated by the fact that they are moving through a profoundly egocentric time in their life. Egocentrism, by definition, means caring only for oneself. To be egocentric is to be self-centered, self-important and self-absorbed.

There is little, if any, room for "other" in the egocentric worlds of children and adolescents. As such, achieving their goals, whatever those might be, are of paramount concern to the child and adolescent. Who or what ever blocks the achievement of their self-centered goals becomes, therefore, the object of their anger. Rewarding the egocentrism of children and adolescents, by giving in to their angry outbursts, does not further the goal of helping them live in the real world where the wishes of others also need to be taken into consideration. As a matter of fact, giving in to their anger actually retards their growth. To stand firm in the face of their angry demands requires that you first understand the nature of your own anger and then resist either capitulating or retaliating against them.

Another possible explanation for the anger expressed by children and adolescents may be related to their understanding of how limited their *resources* are when compared to those possessed by adults. Children and adolescents are painfully aware of their inability to meet almost all of their basic needs. Ten year-old Sally knows she can't get the keys to the car, drive to McDonald's, and buy herself a hamburger. Nor could she pay for the clothes she wears, or for the concert tickets she bought last week. To achieve almost any goal, or acquire almost any material good, she must either enlist, or try coercing, her parents. To the extent that her parents give in to her angry demands, they reinforce and reward her anger.

Given that their resources are limited, this means that children and adolescents have substantially less *power* than the adults around them do. Anger may serve as a means of clawing back some of the power adults have and, in that respect, may be seen by children and adolescents as a way of leveling the playing field. As noted earlier, anger gives people, including children and adolescents, the sense of being more powerful and potent than they really are. In this respect the child's anger may make him or her feel more powerful in dealing with the adult world.

Finally, it appears that children and adolescents have a *compressed sense of time* based upon their limited experiences with the world. They are masters of what others have called "low-frustration tolerance" or LFT. They believe that they *must* get everything they demand *immediately* because, to delay getting it, means waiting for what seems to be an agonizingly long period of time. How often have you told your child that he or she would need to wait until the weekend in order to visit the mall, only to hear their predictably dramatic response, "But I can't wait *that long*!" Tomorrow is an eternity to children and they will anger and frustrate themselves greatly when they do not get what they want, when they think they *should, must* and *ought to* get it!

HELPING ANGRY CHILDREN AND ADOLESCENTS:
POSSIBLE SOLUTIONS

Before commercial airliners take off, passengers are instructed as to the safety features and procedures for the aircraft. One procedure involves placing an oxygen mask over your face should the cabin lose pressure. When travelling with someone who is either too young, too old, or too ill to care for themselves, whose mask are you instructed to put on first – yours or the person's you are travelling with? The correct answer is to put yours on first since, if you do not take care of yourself, you will of little help to the other person. It is the same way when trying to help your child or adolescent deal with his or her anger. You must first take care of your own anger before you are in a position to help them take care of theirs.

Not surprisingly, helping your child or adolescent gain control of their anger requires that you first gain control of yours! Practice the ABC's of REBT in front of them. When you anger yourself which, hopefully, you will be doing less of by now, show them how you work through a "Managing Your Anger" worksheet. Enlist their help in working through this process so they become familiar with it. Talk to them about the ways anger has interfered with your life, especially your important relationships, and why it is that you now want to experience less of it in your life. Let them see how you are dealing with your anger in new, more helpful ways. *Never* reinforce the notion that other people make you angry. Be very careful about the language you use in front of children and adolescents. Never say that, "So-in-so made me so angry today!" rather, phrase it this way, "I really *chose* to make myself angry over what so-in-so did today!" By accepting responsibility for the creation of your own anger, you get them to at least consider the notion that they create their own anger. In short, practice what you preach by teaching your children and adolescents a new language that helps them understand and deal with their emotions and behaviors.

Teach children and adolescents that they *create and control* their emotions based on how they *think* about certain situations. One way to get them to understand this concept is by using teaching stories. Ed Nottingham, Ph.D., is fond of using the following story with his clients. For your purposes, simply substitute your child or adolescent for the client. Dr. Nottingham asks his client to imagine standing in line at McDonald's after a particularly unpleasant day at work (you may want to substitute school for work). The client is very tired and the line ahead of him is painfully long and slow moving. The client looks up at the menu when, all of a sudden, there is a sharp tap in the middle of his back. Without turning around, he begins getting angry. Thoughts like, "He *should* be more considerate!" and "He *should* watch what he is doing!" begin filling the client's head. The tapping continues for another minute or two until the client has so angered himself that he turns around to "let the other person have it." At which point he realizes that the person tapping him on the back is blind and doing so by mistake. Given this new information, how does the client feel? Sad? Ashamed? Guilty? Possibly, but certainly no longer angry. Where has the anger gone? The person kept on tapping, yet the client's anger dissipated because how he *thinks* about being tapped has changed. There are countless stories you could use to illustrate the point that changing the way you think about something leads to changes in how you feel about it. Recounting personal experiences where your feelings changed because your thinking changed would be a very powerful lesson for your young listeners.

Discuss with them the differences between the "World of Should" and the "World of Is" as found in Chapter Three. Some children and adolescents are capable of understanding that there is a difference between the way they think the world *should be,* and the way it *really is.* This gives you an opportunity to discuss the twin notions of *fairness* and *unfairness.* Children and adolescents have very strong views about what constitutes fair and unfair treatment. Help them understand that the belief, "Life must always be fair" has no support in your experience and that, in reality, life is oftentimes unfair. Help them understand that the question before them, when confronted by unfairness, really becomes how they *choose* to respond to that unfairness. Will they anger themselves, thereby increasing the likelihood that they will do or say something that causes them further problems? Or will they irritate themselves in the face of the unfairness thereby motivating themselves to find a way to redress their concerns?

> *Being treated fairly or unfairly is something over which we have no control. How we choose to respond to such treatment is something over which we have total control! We are not guaranteed anything in life.*

To the extent possible, help children and adolescents use humor to challenge their anger-producing beliefs. This is not the same as making fun of their anger-producing beliefs. Rather, this involves getting them to articulate their beliefs and then asking them to step back and evaluate how sensible they are. If you can get them to act out dramatically their anger-producing beliefs, like I did in the example where I was late for an appointment and stuck in traffic, so much the better. The object of the exercise is to get them to recognize how foolish their anger-producing beliefs really are.

Though it requires that they work against their egocentric tendencies, find ways to help them learn to empathize with others. The Empathic Interview is one technique you could use. Have them interview you after one of their angry episodes so they get to know how you view being on the receiving end of their anger. Offer to let them conduct the same interview with you, after you get angry with them, so you will understand how they experience your anger.

Teach them how to take a PTO. This may be the first thing you want your child or adolescent to learn to help them better manage their anger. The steps involved in taking a PTO are detailed in Chapter Four. Review those steps with your child. Have them pay particular attention to the physiological and behavioral cues that reliably precede their anger. Train them to view those physiological and/or behavioral cues as "warning signs" that they are about to explode angrily with all the negative consequences such an explosion entails.

Appeal to their self-interest by pointing out that they will get more of the "stuff" they like by not getting angry, and less of it by getting angry. One colleague views children and adolescents as "tiny business people." That is, they are constantly seeking ways to get more of what they want from the adults around them. By reinforcing their non-angry, non-aggressive responses, they learn that they get more by responding this way then they did by getting angry.

Lastly, help them understand that there is no such thing as unconditional love-- including the love between a parent and a child. Needless to say, this is a very controversial notion and one which women (including my wife!) have trouble agreeing with. The idea I wish to communicate here goes something like this. While the love between you and your child may be *qualitatively different* than the love between you and your wife, or between you and a friend, the need to establish certain *boundaries or limits* for that love are just as important as they are in your other relationships. It is understandable that the amount of "latitude" you might grant your child is far greater than what might be granted others. That there would be no outermost boundary or limit to your love, such that the child would not fear crossing that boundary, has many problems associated with it. Children need to understand that while your love for them is flexible to a degree others do not enjoy, *it is not infinitely flexible* and is capable of breaking beyond repair based on their behavior.

SUGGESTED HOMEWORK:

A.)   Complete one "Managing Your Anger" form as found in the Appendix.

B.)   Complete one "Assertiveness Worksheet" as found in the Appendix.

C.)   The next time your child gets angry with you, help him or her complete the "Empathic Interview" form as found in the Appendix. A completed example is supplied.

D.)   The next time your child gets angry with you, help him or her complete the "Cost-Benefit Analysis" form as found in the Appendix.

CHAPTER TEN

ANGER AND YOUR PAST

The greatest discovery of my generation is that a human being can alter his life by altering his attitude.

William James

The wife of a prospective client called to arrange therapy for her husband regarding his explosive anger. She began the conversation by noting that he had changed over the course of their three-year marriage and become verbally abusive towards her. In addition to her concerns over whether his verbal aggression would escalate into physical aggression, she expressed the fear that her young son would grow up having a "temper like his father." As we discussed her husband's previous failed efforts at treatment, she offered the following observation, "I think what really makes my husband angry is how he was treated as a child. His father was a very angry man who verbally and psychologically abused all his children." At that point I stopped our conversation and asked her, as I am now asking you, to consider the following observations.

When compared with other fields of study, the history of psychiatry is relatively brief. Briefer still is the history of psychology. During that short history, however, certain *myths* have developed surrounding both psychiatry and psychology that do a disservice to the very people we as professionals are charged with helping. The first myth requires that therapy, if it is to be successful, involve an exploration and resolution of past issues. The second myth requires that this process of exploration and resolution be both time-consuming and costly. The popular media feed into these myths by portraying forms of therapy more characteristic of the 1940's and 50's than what is common during the last decade of the twentieth century. The movie star and director Woody Allen is the best example possible of this bizarre relationship between the film industry, and other media, and their advancement of what is really turn of the 19th century Freudian psychiatry!

Since the late 1950's, psychology has developed a number of new techniques for dealing with the full range of human psychological problems, including clinical depression, extreme anxiety and, to a lesser extent, anger. What is important for you to know, as the consumer of these services, is that these new techniques *do not require that you to retreat into your past in order to find solutions for your present. You are not a prisoner of your past!* Nor do you have to go through years of expensive therapy before finding a way to lessen negative emotions like anger. *You can start enjoying a life with less anger today!* You need only follow the guidelines found in this book, which emphasize changing the way you think about the activators in your life (both past and present), in order to experience less anger *right now!* For the wife of the prospective client discussed above to state that her husband's anger in the present is due to events occurring in his childhood is both uninformed and untrue. It is a myth *because all anger is created in the present based on how you think — even about things from your past!*

> *At times clients suggest that what I am really teaching them is "the power of positive thinking." Nothing could be farther from the truth. What they are really learning is the "power of accurate thinking." That is, the power that comes from seeing things as they really are, rather than how the client thinks they should, must, or ought to be. It would be ridiculous for most of us to "think positively" about losing a high paying job we enjoy. Getting angry over that loss, however, is equally unnecessary. By thinking accurately you create emotions, like irritation, that help you solve your problems.*

You have been learning throughout this book that you create your own anger, in the *present*, based on how you think about *current* activators. Simply because an activator occurred in the *past* does not change how your anger in the *present* is formed! You have the tools to resolve anger regardless of whether the activator is a current problem, or one you faced in the distant past. Use your tools!

ANGER AND ABUSE

> *Sylvia is forty-one years old. I had met her two years before while doing a rotation on an inpatient psychiatric unit. She was contacting me now because, "No one else will see me. You are my last hope to deal with my anger." Ten minutes into the session I recalled the details of her problem leading to inpatient treatment. An older brother had sexually abused her for many years. While he currently enjoyed considerable professional success and social prestige, she languished in a series of low paying jobs and had few, if any, friends. Though the actual abuse had stopped over twenty-five years ago, she continued harboring feelings of profound anger towards him because he steadfastly refused to acknowledge that it had taken place. As the session came to an end I suggested to Sylvia that, if she were to "get better," she would ultimately need to abandon her anger toward her brother. Her jet black eyes grew even smaller and she screamed, "You can't possibly expect me <u>not</u> to be angry with my brother for what he did to me! He destroyed my life!" At which point she stormed out of my office and I did not see her again. When a client like Sylvia is allowing anger to destroy her life, and is looking for a therapist to "validate" her anger, I refuse to collaborate in that process.*

That persons suffer various forms of abuse is without question. What is to be done about that abuse, however, from a treatment standpoint, is the source of much controversy. It strikes me that, for the past twenty years or so, our society has come to glorify those who are "victims" of abuse. In the process of glorifying victims an entire industry has developed ostensibly to help these individuals when, in point of fact, it serves only to perpetuate their status as victims. Let me explain what I mean.

To the extent that the "perfect family" has ever existed, it has done so only in books, on TV or in the movies. The notion of the perfect family, or the perfect childhood, is a fiction—albeit a very seductive fiction. The reality is that each of us, to varying degrees, experienced a less than ideal childhood. The treatment of past abuse (be that abuse verbal, physical, psychological or sexual), as prescribed by the "victim industry," dictates that you first "get in touch" with your anger. According to this view, you are perfectly justified in your anger and only by acknowledging and "feeling" your anger will you ever get better. Once you acknowledge your righteous anger, the victim industry requires that you "confront" the abuser and demand that he or she take responsibility for what was done to you.

By now it should be easy for you to recognize the problems with this approach— and they are many! To anger your self in the present, over an activator that took place years ago, is a waste of your precious time and limited psychological resources. The anger you produce in the present in no way alters the past activator and serves only to make you miserable today! As long as you believe that your father, mother, aunt, uncle, brother, sister, neighbor, etc. *makes* you angry because of what they did to you thirty years-ago, who is in control of you? Who is in control of your emotions? Who is the emotional puppet-master and who is the emotional puppet? While you may not like hearing this, the truth remains that your anger in the present simply perpetuates the earlier abuse. Except that, in this case, it will be your anger that continues the abuse!

> *Michelle was abused as a child by her drug addicted parents. The scope of the abuse was almost beyond human comprehension. Toward the end of our work together she said, "Whenever I thought about the abuse I would become so angry I almost couldn't breath. It was like someone was holding my head under water and I was gasping for air. The greatest gift I have given myself in therapy is an understanding that it was really my own hand holding my head under water all that time."*

Overcoming your anger, when the activator is an event that occurred in the past, is accomplished using the same techniques you have been practicing throughout this book. You identify the activator, and then your anger-producing beliefs toward the activator. Disputing your anger-producing beliefs, by asking yourself the various questions as covered in Chapter Two, is the next and likely most daunting step in this entire process. This is especially true because you have been rehearsing these anger-producing beliefs for many years and because you may even have been encouraged to harbor them by ill-informed, albeit well meaning, others—including therapists! After disputing your anger-producing beliefs, you replace them with more effective beliefs emphasizing your *wish* that the activator not have occurred, but recognizing that you had *no control* over the activator. With the new effective beliefs comes a sense of acceptance over what took place and, with that acceptance, comes less anger.

What role does *forgiveness* play in helping to overcome anger directed toward activators from your past? When working with clients, especially those who have been abused, forgiveness comes as the final step in the process of quelling their anger. In many respects, forgiveness is a form of challenge, or disputation, to your anger-producing beliefs. Forgiving the activator allows you to take psychological energy that was being devoted to perpetuating your anger, and thus the abuse, and reallocate it towards more productive ends—like living in the present! *The important thing to remember about forgiveness is not that it is a gift you give the activator; rather, it is a gift you give yourself!*

DISPLACED ANGER

Angela entered therapy for her anger as her wedding date grew nearer. "I know that my anger is a problem in our relationship and I need to do something about it before we get married." As we spoke, she rather dispassionately discussed the lies her deceased father had frequently told her as a child and all the times he had promised her one thing, only to renege on that promise later. She then discussed her relationship with Mike, whose financial past was rather suspect, though he had assured Angela that things were "getting better." When she learned from Mike's parents that things were indeed not getting better financially, Angela exploded in anger and threatened to cancel the wedding. Mike, for his part, couldn't believe her fury and began reconsidering his decision to marry her.

When dealing with issues of abuse and anger, it is easy for the anger intended for the abuser to be expressed towards another. When this occurs, it is referred to as "displaced anger." Anger may be displaced for a variety of reasons. One reason may be that the person who served as the activator for your anger is so powerful that the consequences of getting angry with him or her would be overwhelmingly negative for you. Another explanation is that the activator is no longer available to you for some reason (i.e., he or she has died, relocated, etc.). Whatever the reason, displaced anger can have devastating consequences for your relationships because you are expressing your anger towards someone who played no role in triggering that anger. One way of knowing whether or not your anger is displaced is by assessing its "proportionality." By proportionality I mean that the anger you direct towards another should be proportional to what they either did, or didn't do (the activating event). When your angry response is disproportional to the activating event, that suggests that your anger is being displaced and really ought to be directed towards another. You will know when your angry response is disproportionate to the activating event because the person receiving your anger will often be surprised by its intensity and almost seem to be asking, "What did I do to deserve that?" Training yourself to recognize when you are displacing your anger on to others is not easy and is most likely best accomplished with the assistance of a competent therapist.

BEING GRATEFUL FOR YOUR ACTIVATORS

Shadowlands is a movie I frequently recommend to clients dealing with issues surrounding loss and anger. The story captures the life of the Anglican theologian C. S. Lewis, as portrayed by Anthony Hopkins, at precisely the moment he moves from writing and lecturing in the abstract about the notions of joy and pain, to actually experiencing both. He had successfully avoided both joy and pain, which he viewed as forever connected in the human experience, by steadfastly refusing to allow himself to love another human being. That is until a woman, appropriately enough named Joy, entered his life. What began as a friendship based on her admiration for his many books blossomed into love as Lewis, for the first time, chose to experience the joy associated with loving another. But with joy comes pain and, soon after their marriage, the couple learned that Joy was dying of cancer. Tears of happiness were transformed into tears of anger as Lewis demanded to know of God why Joy was being taken from him. Such was his anger and pain that, at one point, he even questioned his decision to have loved her at all.

Earlier in the book we discussed gratitude as it relates to entitlement based forms of anger. Here we discuss the notion of being *grateful* for the activators in your life. Admittedly, this is not an easy concept to understand, nor is it easy to put into practice. With this in mind, why would I propose to C. S. Lewis, were he my client, that he be grateful for the death of his beloved Joy?

Those of you reading this book that have ever fought in war know that it is one thing to *train for battle*, and another thing entirely to *fight in battle*. The former being a pale imitation of the latter. Only by responding to the real challenges of battle do you understand completely what your capabilities are as a soldier and, ultimately, as a human being. This is the nature of life. Only by welcoming activators into your life, and then solving the problems they present, will you truly learn what you are made of. For C. S. Lewis, the death of Joy served as the most profound activator imaginable for his anger. It shook the very foundations of his world and religious convictions. Yet it was only by struggling with her death, in his own mind, that he was able to overcome the beliefs that brought him such anger and pain. Ultimately, he transformed his anger at her death into sadness, and then once again into joy, by recalling the advice she had given him one afternoon as they huddled in a barn to avoid a pouring rain. Where Lewis, also known as Jack, wanted to avoid the topic of her impending death, Joy knew she had to prepare him for it. "It's not going to last Jack." she said, "But that doesn't spoil it, it just makes it real. What I'm trying to say is that the pain then is part of the happiness now. That's the deal." Without being willing to experience the pain growing out of her death, Lewis would have been unable to experience the joy she brought him in the present. Unless he was willing to be grateful for this activator there literally, and figuratively, would have been no Joy in his life. That *is* the deal!

> *It was Shelly's last night in the group. She is the former Marine nurse we met in Chapter Three whose ten-year-old son had recently been diagnosed with leukemia. Unbeknownst to the other members and myself, Shelly was waiting that night for a page from the hospital where her father-in-law was dying of cancer. Earlier in the session, when asked to summarize her group experiences for one of the new members, she said, "When I first came into this group I was so angry. What got me here was that, about four months ago, I learned that my seventeen-year-old drug-addicted son had relapsed. After all we had been through with him I just couldn't believe it! My husband and I have been married for ten years now and we have a good marriage. When I got home from seeing my son in the hospital that night I just freaked out. I was screaming and crying in the front yard and my husband grabbed my arms and shook me. The neighbors saw that and called 911. This group didn't help me with that problem, because there really was no problem between us. I just didn't know that it was going to help me with all the other problems that were right around the corner. I guess God must have known something I didn't. I'm so grateful for having had this experience."*

We have now come full circle. Yes, life is difficult. Life colored by anger is even more so. At the beginning of Chapter Two I quoted the German philosopher Reinhold Niebuhr who gave the world what has since come to be known as "The Serenity Prayer":

> *God grant me the serenity*
> *to accept the things I cannot change,*
> *courage to change the things I can,*
> *and the wisdom to know the difference.*

I have long been struck by how similar this profound prayer is to many of the ideas I've tried imparting in this book. Were I to recast this prayer ever so slightly it might take this form:

God grant me the serenity
to accept the things I cannot change (the activators in my life),
courage to change the things I can (my own thoughts, feelings and behaviors),
and the wisdom to know the difference.

To those of you who truly understand what this book is all about, and who strive to live according to this prayer, I say, "Congratulations, dear friend, on your newfound serenity."

SUGGESTED HOMEWORK:

A.)   Complete one "Managing Your Anger" form as found in the Appendix.

B.)   Complete one "Assertiveness Worksheet" as found in the Appendix.

C.)   True/False: In order to reduce your anger, so you can live a happier life, you must remain in therapy for at least five years.

D.)   Why would anyone be "grateful for the activators in their life?"_____
_____
_____

E.)   Review this book at least once every six months so you can refresh your understanding of the principles covered.

F.)   Buy a copy of this book and give it to someone you love who is having trouble managing his or her anger. They will thank you many times over.

AFTERWORD

Having never undertaken a project like this before, I am left wondering as to whether or not I achieved the goals originally set for this book. Those goals being to help you to understand where your anger comes from, and how to better manage it. My most sincere hope is that I have been at least moderately successful in both of these areas.

Already I can think of many changes that await a revised edition. Should you wish to pass along suggestions of your own for improving this work, I would warmly welcome them. Please address all correspondence to:

Bradley P. Barris, Ph.D.
5327 McKans Cove
Memphis, TN.   38120
(901) 391-7684

OR

e-mail address: noangerdoc@aol.com

1 August 1999
Memphis, TN.

APPENDIX:

HOMEWORK EXERCISES

MANAGING YOUR ANGER: EXAMPLE

By using the A,B,C's of REBT you can change high levels of anger into more helpful irritation. Use this form soon after you experience an increase in your anger. It will help remind you that only you can create your anger, and that you can change your anger to irritation by changing your anger-producing beliefs.

A. **Activator:** What happened right before you began feeling angry?: My wife invited Sheila over to visit though I have told her not to.

C. **Consequences:** There are three consequences:

a.) **Emotional:** Rate how angry you **felt** on a scale of 0-10. "0" is no anger, while "10" is as angry as you have ever been: I got real angry, about an 8.

b.) **Behaviors:** What did you **do** when you felt angry? I screamed at Sheila to leave, and then I pushed my wife into the kitchen and started yelling at her.

c.) **Physical:** Describe what happened **inside your body** as you got angry: I got to feeling hot, my heart started pounding fast, and my muscles were all tense.

B. **Beliefs:** It is your **commanding beliefs** about the activator, not the activator itself, which causes you to feel and behave in certain ways. What did you **think** to yourself about the activator? Look for words like "should," "must" or "ought." (1) Sheila **should** get out of our house! (2) I don't go against my wife's wishes, so she **shouldn't** go against mine! (3) My wife **should** just do what I tell her to do!

D. **Disputation:** Once you identify your anger-producing beliefs, you need to dispute or challenge them. Ask yourself questions like: Where is it written that...? Does this belief help or hurt me? Does this belief help or hurt the important relationships in my life? Where is it written that my wife **must** do what I tell her to do? Just because I don't go against her wishes doesn't mean that she **must not** go against mine. Holding on to these beliefs **hurt me** and it **hurts our relationship.**

E. **Effective Beliefs:** These are your new beliefs about the activator. They are preferential, help you and your relationships, and recognize that you have **no control** over the activator: I would prefer that my wife not have Sheila over to the house, but I have **no control** over her.

F. **Feelings:** After disputing your beliefs, and replacing them with more effective beliefs, re-rate your level of irritation, describe your new behaviors and what you would experience physically.

New level of irritation would be (0-5): I'd still be irritated with her, about a 3 or 4. New behaviors would be: I would **assertively** discuss the situation with her. My new physical feelings would be: Heart rate slows down, less muscle tension

MANAGING YOUR ANGER

By using the A,B,C's of REBT you can change high levels of anger into more helpful irritation. Use this form soon after you experience an increase in your anger. It will help remind you that only you can create your anger, and that you can change your anger to irritation by changing your anger-producing beliefs.

A.   **Activator:** What happened right before you began feeling angry?:_____
_____

C.   **Consequences:** There are three consequences:

    a.) **Emotional:** Rate how angry you **felt** on a scale of 0-10. "0" is no anger while "10" is as angry as you have ever been:_____

    b.) **Behaviors:** What did you **do** when you felt angry?:_____
_____

    c.) **Physical:** Describe what happened **inside your body** as you got angry: _____
_____

B.   **Beliefs:** It is your **commanding beliefs** about the activator, not the activator itself, which causes you to feel and behave in certain ways. What did you **think** to yourself about the activator? Remember, look for words like "should," "must" or "ought.":_____
_____
_____

D.   **Disputation:** Once you identify your anger-producing beliefs, you need to dispute or challenge them. Ask yourself questions like: Where is it written that...? Does this belief help or hurt me? Does this belief help or hurt the important relationships in my life?_____
_____

H.   **Effective Beliefs:** These are your new beliefs about the activator. They are preferential, help you and your relationships, and recognize that you have **no control** over the activator:_____
_____

F.   **Feelings:** After disputing your beliefs, and then replacing them with more effective beliefs, re-rate your level of <u>irritation</u>, describe your new behaviors and what you would experience physically.

New level of irritation would be (0-5):_____
New behaviors would be:_____
My new physical feelings would be:_____

When Chicken Soup Isn't Enough: Managing Your Anger in an Increasingly Angry World
Bradley P. Barris, Ph.D. This form may be reproduced without the author's permission.

95

MANAGING YOUR ANGER

By using the A,B,C's of REBT you can change high levels of anger into more helpful irritation. Use this form soon after you experience an increase in your anger. It will help remind you that only you can create your anger, and that you can change your anger to irritation by changing your anger-producing beliefs.

A.   **Activator:** What happened right before you began feeling angry?:_____
_____

C.   **Consequences:** There are three consequences:

a.) **Emotional:** Rate how angry you **felt** on a scale of 0-10. "0" is no anger while "10" is as angry as you have ever been:_____

b.) **Behaviors:** What did you **do** when you felt angry?:_____
_____

c.) **Physical:** Describe what happened **inside your body** as you got angry: _____
_____

B.   **Beliefs:** It is your **commanding beliefs** about the activator, not the activator itself that causes you to feel and behave in certain ways. What did you **think** to yourself about the activator? Remember, look for words like "should," "must" or "ought.":_____
_____
_____

D.   **Disputation:** Once you identify your anger-producing beliefs, you need to dispute or challenge them. Ask yourself questions like: Where is it written that...? Does this belief help or hurt me? Does this belief help or hurt the important relationships in my life?_____
_____

I.   **Effective Beliefs:** These are your new beliefs about the activator. They are preferential, help you and your relationships, and recognize that you have **no control** over the activator:_____
_____

F.   **Feelings:** After disputing your beliefs, and then replacing them with more effective beliefs, re-rate your level of <u>irritation</u>, describe your new behaviors and what you would experience physically.

New level of irritation would be (0-5):_____
New behaviors would be:_____
My new physical feelings would be:_____

When Chicken Soup Isn't Enough: Managing Your Anger in an Increasingly Angry World
Bradley P. Barris, Ph.D. This form may be reproduced without the author's permission.

96

ASSERTIVENESS WORKSHEET: EXAMPLE

Assertiveness involves telling the activator what you **think** and **feel** about a particular situation, as well as asking him or her to **do** something for you.

Assertiveness involves the following four steps:

STEP 1.)   Describe the problem situation to the activator (usually the activator's behavior)

THEN

STEP 2.)   Tell the activator how you **choose** to feel about their behavior

THEN

STEP 3.)   Tell the activator how their behavior affects you

THEN

STEP 4.)   Suggest a new behavior of the activator that you would **prefer**

Here is an example based on a situation that occurred recently to me:

STEP 1.)   When you did not call me early in the day as I had asked

STEP 2.)   I **chose** to anger myself

STEP 3.)   Because your failure to call meant I couldn't plan my activities that evening.

STEP 4.)   In the future I would prefer that you call me as soon as possible so I can plan accordingly.

Remember, simply because you assertively ask the activator for something does not mean you will get it. The success in behaving assertively comes from the asking itself! Behaving assertively cannot cause the people to feel anything. If you have resisted behaving assertively because you believed that what you wanted to say would hurt someone's feelings, remind yourself that you are not powerful enough to hurt anyone's feelings. If the other person becomes upset, they have *chosen to upset themselves!*

ASSERTIVENESS WORKSHEET

Assertiveness involves telling the activator what you **think** and **feel** about a particular situation, as well as asking him or her to **do** something for you.

Assertiveness involves the following four steps:

STEP 1.)   Describe the problem situation to the activator (usually the activator's behavior)

THEN

STEP 2.)   Tell the activator how you **choose** to feel about their behavior

THEN

STEP 3.)   Tell the activator how their behavior affects you

THEN

STEP 4.)   Suggest a new behavior of the activator that you would **prefer**

For practice, complete an example based on a situation that occurred recently in your life.

STEP 1.)   When you _____

_____

STEP 2.)   I chose to feel_____

STEP 3.)   Because your behavior _____

_____

STEP 4.)   In the future I would prefer that you _____

_____

Remember, simply because you assertively ask the activator for something does not mean you will get it. The success in behaving assertively comes from the asking itself! Behaving assertively cannot cause the people to feel anything. If you have resisted behaving assertively because you believed that what you wanted to say would hurt someone's feelings, remind yourself that you are not powerful enough to hurt anyone's feelings. If the other person becomes upset, they have *chosen to upset themselves!*

When Chicken Soup Isn't Enough: Managing Your Anger in an Increasingly Angry World
Bradley P. Barris, Ph.D. This form may be reproduced without the author's permission.

ASSERTIVENESS WORKSHEET

Assertiveness involves telling the activator what you **think** and **feel** about a particular situation, as well as asking him or her to **do** something for you.

Assertiveness involves the following four steps:

STEP 1.)   Describe the problem situation to the activator (usually the activator's behavior)

THEN

STEP 2.)   Tell the activator how you **choose** to feel about their behavior

THEN

STEP 3.)   Tell the activator how their behavior affects you

THEN

STEP 4.)   Suggest a new behavior of the activator that you would **prefer**

For practice, complete an example based on a situation that occurred recently in your life.

STEP 1.)   When you _____
            _____

STEP 2.)   I chose to feel_____

STEP 3.)   Because your behavior _____
            _____

STEP 4.)   In the future I would prefer that you _____
            _____

Remember, simply because you assertively ask the activator for something does not mean you will get it. The success in behaving assertively comes from the asking itself! Behaving assertively cannot cause the people to feel anything. If you have resisted behaving assertively because you believed that what you wanted to say would hurt someone's feelings, remind yourself that you are not powerful enough to hurt anyone's feelings. If the other person becomes upset, they have *chosen to upset themselves!*

When Chicken Soup Isn't Enough: Managing Your Anger in an Increasingly Angry World
Bradley P. Barris, Ph.D. This form may be reproduced without the author's permission.

ASSERTIVENESS WORKSHEET

Assertiveness involves telling the activator what you **think** and **feel** about a particular situation, as well as asking him or her to **do** something for you.

Assertiveness involves the following four steps:

STEP 1.)   Describe the problem situation to the activator (usually the activator's behavior)

THEN

STEP 2.)   Tell the activator how you **choose** to feel about their behavior

THEN

STEP 3.)   Tell the activator how their behavior affects you

THEN

STEP 4.)   Suggest a new behavior of the activator that you would **prefer**

For practice, complete an example based on a situation that occurred recently in your life.

STEP 1.)   When you _____
            _____

STEP 2.)   I chose to feel_____

STEP 3.)   Because your behavior _____
            _____

STEP 4.)   In the future I would prefer that you _____
            _____

Remember, simply because you assertively ask the activator for something does not mean you will get it. The success in behaving assertively comes from the asking itself! Behaving assertively cannot cause the people to feel anything. If you have resisted behaving assertively because you believed that what you wanted to say would hurt someone's feelings, remind yourself that you are not powerful enough to hurt anyone's feelings. If the other person becomes upset, they have *chosen to upset themselves!*

When Chicken Soup Isn't Enough: Managing Your Anger in an Increasingly Angry World
Bradley P. Barris, Ph.D. This form may be reproduced without the author's permission.

ASSERTIVENESS WORKSHEET

Assertiveness involves telling the activator what you **think** and **feel** about a particular situation, as well as asking him or her to **do** something for you.

Assertiveness involves the following four steps:

STEP 1.)   Describe the problem situation to the activator (usually the activator's behavior)

THEN

STEP 2.)   Tell the activator how you **choose** to feel about their behavior

THEN

STEP 3.)   Tell the activator how their behavior affects you

THEN

STEP 4.)   Suggest a new behavior of the activator that you would **prefer**

For practice, complete an example based on a situation that occurred recently in your life.

STEP 1.)   When you _____
_____

STEP 2.)   I chose to feel_____

STEP 3.)   Because your behavior _____
_____

STEP 4.)   In the future I would prefer that you _____
_____

Remember, simply because you assertively ask the activator for something does not mean you will get it. The success in behaving assertively comes from the asking itself! Behaving assertively cannot cause the people to feel anything. If you have resisted behaving assertively because you believed that what you wanted to say would hurt someone's feelings, remind yourself that you are not powerful enough to hurt anyone's feelings. If the other person becomes upset, they have *chosen to upset themselves!*

When Chicken Soup Isn't Enough: Managing Your Anger in an Increasingly Angry World
Bradley P. Barris, Ph.D. This form may be reproduced without the author's permission.

PROBLEM SOLVING WORKSHEET-EXAMPLE

Step One: Answer the question "Do I have a problem?"

Emotional Answers   Behavioral Answers   Physical Answers

I am angry all the time.

I am yelling at my wife.

My blood pressure is elevated.

YES

NO → STOP

Step Two: Define the problem by gathering as much information about it as you can: <u>When I ask my wife to run an errand for me she does not always follow though with my request.</u>

Step Three: Brainstorm as many solutions to the problem as possible, *no matter how crazy some of those solutions might initially seem.*
1.) <u>I could get angry with her and make her do the errands correctly.</u>

2.) <u>I will not do any errands for her unless she does mine correctly.</u>
3.) <u>I could leave a list for her with very specific instructions.</u>
4.) <u>I could be more appreciative of the errands she does run for me.</u>

Step Four: Evaluate the solutions from Step Three and keep only those you think will solve the problem without creating new problems.
1.) <u>I could leave a list for her with very specific instructions.</u>
2.) <u>I could be more appreciative of the errands she does run for me.</u>
3.) <u>I could combine solutions 1 & 2 so she is even more likely to run my errands correctly.</u>

Step Five and Beyond: Try the first solution on the list from Step Four. If it solves the problem you are done! If not, go back to the list and try the second solution, and so on. Go back to Step Two and redefine the problem if none of the options at Step Four give you the solution you want.

PROBLEM SOLVING WORKSHEET

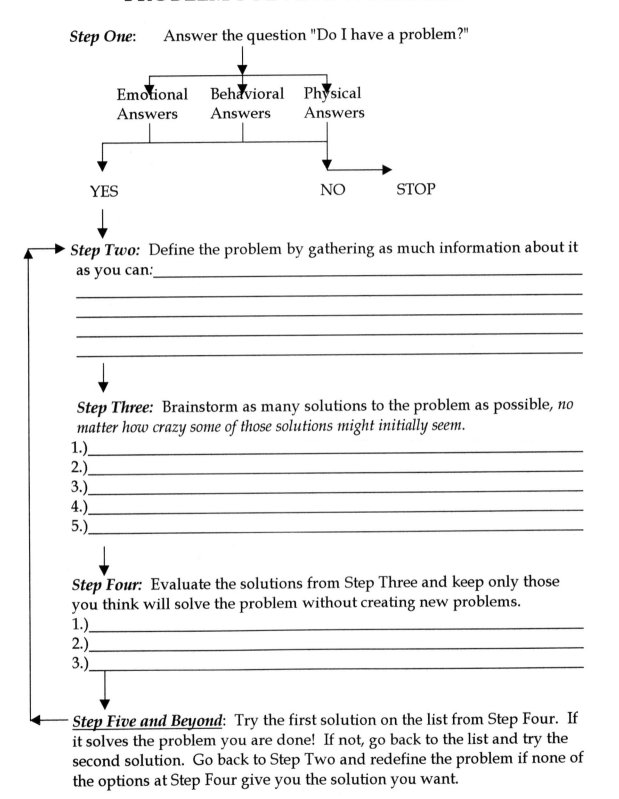

Step One: Answer the question "Do I have a problem?"

Emotional   Behavioral   Physical
Answers   Answers   Answers

YES   NO   STOP

Step Two: Define the problem by gathering as much information about it as you can:_____

_____
_____
_____
_____

Step Three: Brainstorm as many solutions to the problem as possible, *no matter how crazy some of those solutions might initially seem.*

1.)_____
2.)_____
3.)_____
4.)_____
5.)_____

Step Four: Evaluate the solutions from Step Three and keep only those you think will solve the problem without creating new problems.

1.)_____
2.)_____
3.)_____

Step Five and Beyond: Try the first solution on the list from Step Four. If it solves the problem you are done! If not, go back to the list and try the second solution. Go back to Step Two and redefine the problem if none of the options at Step Four give you the solution you want.

When Chicken Soup Isn't Enough: Managing Your Anger in an Increasingly Angry World
Bradley P. Barris, Ph.D. This form may be reproduced without the author's permission.

103

COST-BENEFIT ANALYSIS: EXAMPLE

Most people believe that getting angry helps them get what they demand. I've been teaching you that, *in almost all cases*, getting angry is not in your long-term best interests. Which view is correct? One way to answer this question is by doing a Cost-Benefit analysis of the situation where you angered yourself. In this exercise you are asked to list the benefits of getting angry, along with the costs. Make sure you record *both the short and long-term consequences of your anger.*

Situation you angered yourself about: I angered myself the other day when my wife didn't pick up my laundry from the cleaners like she said she would.

Anger-producing belief: She should have kept her promise and gotten my laundry.

BENEFITS OF GETTING ANGRY	COSTS OF GETTING ANGRY
Short-Term Benefits:	Short-Term Costs:
1.) My wife got into the car and picked my clothes up from the laundry though it was getting pretty late.	1.) My wife was very tired when she got back and pretty upset with me for having gotten so angry.
2.) I had clean clothes to wear to the office the next day for my big presentation.	2.) She gave me the "silent treatment" for the next two days.
Long-Term Benefits:	Long-Term Costs:
1.) I can't think of any.	1.) My wife seems more resentful of me than she did before this incident.
2.)	2.) Every so often, I think she "accidentally on purpose" forgets to do other things I ask of her—though she denies that.
3.)	

104

COST-BENEFIT ANALYSIS

Most people believe that getting angry helps them get what they demand. I've been teaching you that, *in almost all cases*, getting angry is not in your long-term best interests. Which view is correct? One way to answer this question is by doing a Cost-Benefit analysis of the situation where you angered yourself. In this exercise you are asked to list the benefits of getting angry, along with the costs. Make sure you record *both the short and long-term consequences of your anger.*

Situation you angered yourself about: _____

_____ :

Anger-producing belief: _____ .

BENEFITS OF GETTING ANGRY	COSTS OF GETTING ANGRY
Short-Term Benefits:	Short-Term Costs:
1.)	1.)
2.)	2.)
Long-Term Benefits:	Long-Term Costs:
1.)	1.)
2.)	2.)

When Chicken Soup Isn't Enough: Managing Your Anger in an Increasingly Angry World
Bradley P. Barris, Ph.D. This form may be reproduced without the author's permission.

TAKING A POLL: EXAMPLE

Whenever my wife and I discuss one of my anger-producing beliefs, her automatic response is, "Well, let's take a poll and see if that's true." The goal of taking a poll is to see whether others view your beliefs to be as valid as you do. Taking a poll gives you feedback concerning how realistic your beliefs are, as seen through the eyes of others. In this exercise you are to identify an anger-producing belief (e.g., "Bosses *must* always treat their employees fairly!") and then ask at least two other people what they think about the validity of that belief. We all know people who anger themselves easily because they see things just like we do. It would be helpful to avoid those people and seek out, instead, people who respond to things more calmly because they have views different from your own. At the end of this exercise record your new belief based on the feedback you've received.

The anger-producing belief I want to take a poll on is: "When I was a child, I *always* did what my parents told me to do, the first time they told me to do it! My kids *should* do the same thing!"

What friend number one said about my anger-producing belief: "I've taught several Sunday school classes full of children over the years and I don't remember one of those children always doing what they were asked to do the first time they were asked. I bet your parents don't remember your behavior the same way you do!"

What friend number two said about my anger-producing belief: "You know, I think I have two pretty good kids and I can tell you that it would be expecting too much of them to always do what I ask of them, the moment I ask it of them. It would be nice if they did, but they're human's like you and me and bound to make mistakes."

My new belief about this situation is: "My friends are probably right. I didn't do everything the first time my parents told me to and it's not realistic to expect that of my children. Also, the angrier I get at them, the more afraid of me they become and that is hurting our relationship. I need to work on myself first, and then work on disciplining them."

TAKING A POLL

Whenever my wife and I discuss one of my anger-producing beliefs, her automatic response is, "Well, let's take a poll and see if that's true." The goal of taking a poll is to see whether others view your beliefs to be as valid as you do. Taking a poll gives you feedback concerning how realistic your beliefs are, as seen through the eyes of others. In this exercise you are to identify an anger-producing belief (e.g., "Bosses *must* always treat their employees fairly!") and then ask at least two other people what they think about the validity of that belief. We all know people who anger themselves easily because they see things just like we do. It would be helpful to avoid those people and seek out, instead, people who respond to things more calmly because they have views different from your own. At the end of this exercise record your new belief based on the feedback you've received.

The anger-producing belief I want to take a poll on is: "_____
_____
_____

What friend number one said about my anger-producing belief: _____
_____
_____
_____
_____

What friend number two said about my anger-producing belief: _____
_____
_____
_____
_____

My new belief about this situation is: _____
_____
_____
_____
_____

When Chicken Soup Isn't Enough: Managing Your Anger in an Increasingly Angry World
Bradley P. Barris, Ph.D. This form may be reproduced without the author's permission.

THE EMPATHIC INTERVIEW: EXAMPLE

Empathy is the ability to put yourself "in another other persons shoes." The "Empathic Interview" is designed to help you understand how other people think and feel when confronted with your anger, and why they choose to behave as they do. In this exercise, you are to interview one person you recently expressed anger towards. As you ask them questions, try empathizing or understanding exactly how they experienced your anger. The better you become at this exercise, the less likely you will be to express anger toward them in the future.

With whom did you anger yourself? I got angry with my father the other day for not taking me shopping like he said he would.

Ask the person you expressed your anger towards how *you* appeared to them. Have them describe your facial expressions, your voice, your "body language," etc.: My dad said that I had kind of a wild look in my eyes. My face was all red and my eyes were almost bulging out. He said that my voice got real loud and that I was screaming at him to take me shopping. He noticed that my fists were balled up and, for a moment, he thought I might try to hit him.

Ask the person you expressed your anger towards how they *felt* toward you. My dad said that at first he felt scared of me, since he thought I might try to punch him. Then he noticed that he was getting angry with me for carrying on like a baby. Then he felt disappointed in me for carrying on so long.

Ask the person you expressed your anger towards to describe what they either said or did, or didn't say or do, as they received your anger. After listening to this for a while dad just looked at me, shook his head, and walked off. Later, when we talked about this situation, he said that he wanted to wanted to tell me how disappointed he was in me for reacting so angrily.

Ask the person you expressed your anger toward whether they were more, or less, likely to do what you were demanding of them after receiving your anger. Dad made it very clear to me that getting angry with him was not the way to get him to take me shopping.

Ask the person you expressed your anger towards to tell you whether they felt closer to you, or more distant, after receiving your anger. Dad also made it clear to me that, when I get angry at him like I did, it really hurts our relationship and that it takes him at least a couple of days to begin feeling close to me again.

THE EMPATHIC INTERVIEW

Empathy is the ability to put yourself "in another other persons shoes." The "Empathic Interview" is designed to help you understand how other people think and feel when confronted with your anger, and why they choose to behave as they do. In this exercise, you are to interview one person you recently expressed anger towards. As you ask them questions, try empathizing or understanding exactly how they experienced your anger. The better you become at this exercise, the less likely you will be to express anger toward them in the future.

With whom did you anger yourself?_____
_____
_____
_____

Ask the person you expressed your anger towards how *you* appeared to them. Have them describe your facial expressions, your voice, your "body language," etc.:_____
_____
_____

Ask the person you expressed your anger towards how they *felt* toward you.____
_____
_____

Ask the person you expressed your anger towards to describe what they either said or did, or didn't say or do, as they received your anger._____
_____
_____

Ask the person you expressed your anger toward whether they were more, or less, likely to do what you were demanding of them after receiving your anger.__
_____
_____

Ask the person you expressed your anger towards to tell you whether they felt closer to you, or more distant, after receiving your anger._____
_____
_____

When Chicken Soup Isn't Enough: Managing Your Anger in an Increasingly Angry World
Bradley P. Barris, Ph.D. This form may be reproduced without the author's permission.

FURTHER READINGS

1.)   Barlow, David H. & Craske, Michelle G. *Mastery of Your Anxiety and Panic II.* Center for Stress and Anxiety Disorders, University of Albany, State University of New York, 1994.

2.)   Bennett, William. *The Book of Virtues.* New York, NY: Simon & Schuster, 1993.

3.)   Bernard, Michael E. & DiGiuseppe, Raymond. *Inside Rational-Emotive Therapy: A Critical Appraisal of the Theory and Therapy of Albert Ellis.* New York, NY: Academic Press, 1989.

4.)   Covey, Stephen R. *The Seven Habits of Highly Effective People.* New York, NY: Simon & Schuster, 1989.

5.)   Ellis, Albert E. *Anger. How to Live with It and Without It.* New York, NY: Citadel Press, 1977.

6.)   Ellis, Albert E. & Dryden, Windy. *The Practice of Rational-Emotive Therapy.* New York, NY: Springer, 1987.

7.)   Hauck, Paul A. *The Three Faces of Love.* Philadelphia, PA.: The Westminster Press, 1984.

8.)   Kassinove, Howard (Ed.). *Anger Disorders: Definition, Diagnosis, And Treatment.* London, Taylor & Francis, 1995.

9.)   Kushner, Harold S. *When Bad Things Happen To Good People.* New York, NY: Avon Books, 1981.

10.)   Lichstein, Kenneth L. *Clinical Relaxation Strategies.* New York, Wiley & Sons, 1988.

11.)   Nottingham, Edgar J. *It's Not As Bad As It Seems: A Thinking Straight Approach to Happiness.* Memphis, TN: Castle Books, 1994.

12.)   Peck, M. Scott. *The Road Less Traveled.* New York, NY: Simon & Schuster, 1978.

ABOUT THE AUTHOR

Bradley P. Barris, Ph.D. holds a doctorate in Clinical Psychology from the University of Memphis. He pursues a multifaceted practice that includes serving as the Director of Psychology at North Mississippi State Hospital, Executive Director of the Center for the Study and Treatment of Anger Related Disorders, and senior partner in *Barris & Associates*. *Barris & Associates* is a consulting firm that works with businesses, schools and police departments teaching their personnel how to better manage anger in the workplace. *Barris & Associates* also work in conjunction with public and private probation organizations in the provision of treatment for domestic violence batterers. As a lecturer for *Mind Matters* and *CorText* seminars, Dr. Barris has trained thousands of mental health professionals across the country in the treatment of angry clients and batterers. He is licensed to practice psychology in Tennessee, Mississippi and Arkansas.

Dear Dr. Barris,

I attended your seminar on "Understanding Anger" in New Orleans in November. I have gone through the last 22 years of my life being "hurt," and eventually "angry." I do not have a hostile or aggressive personality towards others, I have been just so "disappointed" in people. Because of my life experiences, I know that all of your insights are absolutely accurate. I was thrilled to get a clear understanding of what I could do to help myself manage my feelings towards "aggressive people." It is so freeing to know that I have zero control over them. I have wasted so much of my voice, time, emotions, and life trying to "change things for the better." I've talked for hours, days trying to get another to be understanding, caring, etc., etc. I feel I was also trying to control, but for the betterment of all concerned.

I have no further suggestions, but just want to congratulate you on your accomplishments and to thank you so very much. This book is "God-sent." I've never written to anyone like this before, but wanted to express to you how wonderful your book is.

Sincerely,

Lisa M.
New Orleans, LA